CACHE LEVEL 1

The Oldham College

D0714904

# Caring for Children

## AWARD/CERTIFICATE/DIPLOMA

OLDHAM COLLEGE

Renew

te
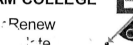

Corinne Barker

Emma Ward

HODDER
EDUCATION
AN HACHETTE UK COMPANY

**OLDHAM COLLEGE**

BARCODE....O56948............

CLASS No...372.21 BAR........

DATE.......Oct 2011...........

Orders: please contact Bookpoint Ltd, 130 Milton Park, Abingdon, Oxon OX14 4SB. Telephone: (44) 01235 827720. Fax: (44) 01235 400454. Lines are open from 9.00–5.00, Monday to Saturday, with a 24-hour message answering service. You can also order through our website www.hoddereducation.co.uk

*British Library Cataloguing in Publication Data*
A catalogue record for this title is available from the British Library

ISBN: 978 1 4441 5148 0

This Edition Published 2011
Impression number   10 9 8 7 6 5 4 3 2 1
Year                          2014, 2013, 2012, 2011

Copyright © 2011 Corinne Barker and Emma Ward

All rights reserved. No part of this publication may be reproduced or transmitted in any form or by any means, electronic or mechanical, including photocopy, recording, or any information storage and retrieval system, without permission in writing from the publisher or under licence from the Copyright Licensing Agency Limited. Further details of such licences (for reprographic reproduction) may be obtained from the Copyright Licensing Agency Limited, of Saffron House, 6-10 Kirby Street, London EC1N 8TS.

Hachette UK's policy is to use papers that are natural, renewable and recyclable products and made from wood grown in sustainable forests. The logging and manufacturing processes are expected to conform to the environmental regulations of the country of origin.

Cover photo: brushing teeth © soupstock–Fotolia.
Typeset by Pantek Media, Maidstone, Kent.
Printed in Italy for Hodder Education, an Hachette UK Company, 338 Euston Road, London NW1 3BH.

# Contents

# Acknowledgements

We would like to dedicate this book to our delightful children who have been so supportive and understanding.

To my lovely daughter Stevie and goddaughter Juliette: thank you for all the treasured memories of you growing up - many happy times have come to mind as I have been writing this book.

Thanks also to my colleagues in the 6th Form Care and Early Years department at Wakefield College for all their support and encouragement, and to all the students I have had the pleasure of teaching – you are the ones that inspire me! – **Corinne Barker**

To the wonderful Jake and the delightful Eva: many thanks for being you! And to Carl - without your support and patience we would not have achieved this - thank you so much.

Thanks also to all the students I have known and taught over the years. You have all been close to mind as I have debated over the words on the page. – **Emma Ward**

We would both like to thank Ann for the words of encouragement, the opportunities she has given us, and for her friendship.

We would like to thank Colin Goodlad at Hodder Education, and Llinos Edwards, for their hard work and support during the writing of this book.

Every effort has been made to trace the copyright holders of material reproduced here. The authors and publishers would like to thank the following for permission to reproduce copyright illustrations:

ABC & 123 blocks © iofoto/Fotolia, except p.2, p.54 & p.106 © Edyta Pawlowska/Fotolia.

P.2 (bottom) © Wichittra Srisunon/Fotolia; p.3 (top) © Ion Popa/Fotolia, (bottom) © Justin O'Hanlon; p.4 (top) © David Bates/Philip Allan, (middle) © JJAVA/Fotolia; p.8 © Beboy/Fotolia; p.9 © Luxian/Fotolia; p.12 © Ala/Fotolia; p.21 © NiDerLander/Fotolia; p.23 © Matthew Cole/Fotolia; p.25 © Zubada/Fotolia; p.27 © NiDerLander/Fotolia; p.29 © Lorelyn Medina/Fotolia; p.31 © Andrew Callaghan; p.35 © Marzanna Syncerz/Fotolia; p.36 © James Steidl/SuperFusion/SuperStock; p.37 © Photosindia.com/SuperStock; p.39 © Corbis/SuperStock; p.40 © Rayman/Digital Vision/Getty Images; p.42 © Konstantin Yuganov/Fotolia; p.46 © Andrew Callaghan; p.51 © Alexander Raths/ Fotolia; p.54 (bottom) © jazzerup/Fotolia; p.59 © picsfive/Fotolia; p.60 © JJAVA/Fotolia; p.61 © nyul/Fotolia; p.64 (bottom) © Beboy/Fotolia; p.66 © Andrew Callaghan; p.67 © Irina Fischer/Fotolia; p.69 © Andrew Callaghan; p.73 © Ilya Postnikov/Fotolia.com; p.75 © Ljupco Smokovski/Fotolia; p.79 (top) © Andrew Callaghan, (bottom) © nyul/Fotolia; p.81 © Courtesy Bede Academy, Blyth, Northumberland; p.82 © Lorelyn Medina/ Fotolia; p.86 © dinostock/Fotolia; p.87 (photo) © Robert Byron/Fotolia; p.89 © Maxim Pavlov/Fotolia; p.91 © Andrey Kisel/Fotolia; p.95 © emel82/Fotolia; p.96 © Speedfighter/Fotolia; p.99 © Lorelyn Medina/Fotolia; p.101 (top) © Sebastian Duda/ Fotolia, (bottom) © Hans-Jürgen Krahl/Fotolia; p.104 © Andrew Callaghan; p.106 (bottom) © HaywireMedia/Fotolia; p.109 © Andrew Callaghan; p.112 © B4Step/Fotolia; p.116 © piai/Fotolia; p.119 © Justin O'Hanlon; p.123 © lordalea/Fotolia; p.126 © Brenda Carson/Fotolia; p.127 © kmit/Fotolia; p.128 © Elenathewise/Fotolia; p.130 (top) © helix/ Fotolia, (bottom) © fox17/Fotolia; p.131 © Crown copyright material as reproduced with the permission of the Controller of HMSO and the Queen's Printer for Scotland; p.132 © Marina Lvova/Fotolia; p.134 © Garo/Phanie/Rex Features; p.139 © hitdelight/ Fotolia; p.140 © Monkey Business/Fotolia; p.142 © Rebecca Abell/Fotolia; p.144 © Robert Harding Picture Library/SuperStock; p.145 © 2004 Alan Carey/The Image Works/TopFoto; p.146 © Irochka/Fotolia; p.150 © Stocksnapper/Fotolia; p.152 (top) © Andrew Callaghan, (bottom) © Justin O'Hanlon; p.153 © Stefan Andronache/Fotolia; p.154 © Andrew Callaghan; p.157 © Andrew Callaghan; p.158 (top) © Justin O'Hanlon, (bottom) © Apple/Fotolia; p.160 © Lorelyn Medina/Fotolia.

# Guide to the book

## What you will learn in this unit

Appearing at the beginning of each chapter, this box tells you what you will learn in the chapter.

**1.1** These circles help you to see which of the assessment criteria is being covered on each page.

## Important words

These boxes explain the meaning of the words you will need to know for the qualification.

## Example!

These boxes will give you examples of what is being discussed on the page.

## Task

These boxes suggest things you can do to help you to understand the subjects that have been explained on the page. For example, you may be asked to discuss the subjects in pairs or as part of a group.

## Assessment task ✔

These boxes describe work which if completed will contribute towards your Evidence Record which will allow you to pass the qualification.

## Summary

This box appears at the end of each chapter, and reminds you of what you should have learnt from reading the chapter.

# Chapter 1

# CFC 13 Sharing learning experiences with children

## What you will learn in this unit

You will gain an understanding of:
- the ways in which children learn
- how to use stories and rhymes with young children
- how exploring the natural world can support children's learning
- ways in which the local community can give children different experiences.

## How children learn 1.1

### Ways in which children learn

**Observation**

This happens when children watch what is happening around them. They will often watch other children playing a game or doing an activity, and perhaps want to join in.

Children like to watch adults doing tasks such as cooking the dinner, baking a cake or putting on make-up. They will often copy what they have seen by using role play.

## Experimenting

This is when children test their skills and understanding. They will often carry out simple experiments to see how things work or what might happen.

Children may experiment by dropping objects into water to see if they float or sink to the bottom. During bath time children often experiment with bubbles or floating toys.

Outside they may also enjoy planting seeds to find out how vegetables and flowers grow.

**Important words**

**Observe** – look at or watch.

## Imaginative and creative play

This happens when children use their own imagination to create a make-believe world. For example, children could pretend to be a vet or a pirate, or act out a story, perhaps using small characters or animals.

Some children enjoy being creative with dough or clay. They have the chance to make models or shapes, or simply enjoy exploring using their senses. When painting during a messy play session, some children really enjoy using a range of paints and materials. This is a good opportunity for them to use their own imagination and experience different textures.

**Figure 1.1** Playdough can encourage children to use their imagination

# How children use their senses to explore the world 1.2

| Sense | How the sense is used |
|---|---|
| Sight | Children use sight to observe the world around them, to see what everything looks like; e.g. children quickly learn to recognise people, objects and places. |
| Hearing | Children listen to and recognise sounds; e.g. a very young baby will recognise the voice of their main carer. Older children can identify animals through the noise they make. |
| Touch | Children investigate using touch to find out what things feel like. By touching, children can experience different textures; e.g. some children may not like the texture of sand or seaweed under their feet when they are walking on the beach. |
| Smell | Children use this sense to experience pleasant or unpleasant smells; e.g. children may recognise what is cooking by the smell in the air, or a person by the perfume they wear. |
| Taste | Children use their sense of taste to discover different flavours; e.g. some children like sweet tastes while others prefer spicy foods. |

**Table 1.1** How children use their senses to explore

## Important words

**Senses** – touch, smell, taste, sight and hearing: used to make sense of the world around us.

**Investigate** – find out (about something).

## Task

**Mai is going to the supermarket with her grandma.**

In pairs, discuss and list the ways that Mai will use her senses to investigate how things look, smell and feel in the supermarket.

*For example*, Mai might use her sense of sight to look at the different colours on the packets and boxes.

## Assessment task 1

Design a poster showing how children use their senses to find out about the world around them. Include sight, taste/smell, hearing and touch in your poster. The poster should show three reasons why it is important for children to find out about the world around them.

## The importance of investigation for children's learning 1.3

Children learn by investigating the world around them. They do this by using all of their senses.

Children need lots of opportunities to learn through investigation. They may need adults around them to provide these opportunities.

Children learn more when they try things out for themselves rather than observing other people doing activities or watching the television.

**Our senses are:**
sight,
hearing,
touch,
taste,
smell.

**Figure 1.2** Children learn through their senses

### Example!

Aadi will enjoy watching Mai completing a jigsaw, but will learn more about shape and size by trying to fit the pieces of jigsaw together by himself.

Children learn by using their senses to investigate the world around them. Through investigation children learn how things work, what things do and why things happen.

Children may learn how to keep themselves safe through investigation: a child could learn that if they walk along a log or wooden beam they must tread carefully to help them balance.

Through investigation children learn about living things, such as how fish swim in water, how a frog jumps or how plants and flowers grow.

## Sharing stories and rhymes 2.1 2.2 2.3

Many stories and rhymes enjoyed by children can support their learning. Adults can use sensory aids with the rhymes and stories to encourage children to join in. Table 1.2 gives examples of sensory aids to use with different rhymes and stories, so that children are encouraged to take part in the activity.

### Important words

**Sensory aid** – objects or materials used by children to encourage the use of their senses when learning.

| Story or rhyme | Sensory aid | Ways to encourage children to take part |
|---|---|---|
| Handa's surprise | A basket full of the fruit used in the story | Children can touch, smell and taste the fruit, learning the names of the fruit and where it grows |
| | Animal masks | Children can enjoy pretending to be the animals in the story |
| | A map of the area in Africa that Handa lives. | The map can be used to show where the story takes place. The children can learn new things about a different country |
| | | These aids can be left in the role play area to encourage children to retell the story later. |
| *The Very Hungry Caterpillar* | A storyboard showing the life cycle of a butterfly: e.g. caterpillar hatches and eats a lot of food, then caterpillar slowly changes into a beautiful butterfly that flies away. | Children can use the storyboard to see the life cycle of the butterfly. |
| | Pictures of food or actual food the caterpillar might enjoy. | Children can taste and smell the food to see which they think the caterpillar will enjoy most. |
| Twinkle, twinkle little star | Different shapes in a feely box or drawstring bag. | Put the shapes in a box or bag and ask the children to close their eyes, feel the shapes and pick out a star shape. |
| | A range of materials: silky, shiny, sparkly, glittery. | Give children the materials, encourage them to investigate the textures and describe what they all feel like. |
| | A collection of musical instruments. | Share out the instruments and allow children to experiment with bells and chimes. |
| Old McDonald had a farm | A sounds CD with different animal noises. | Play the CD and see if the children can recognise the animal sounds. |
| | Animal glove puppets. | Use the glove puppets at appropriate points in the song alongside the CD. |

**Table 1.2** Using sensory aids to support children's learning

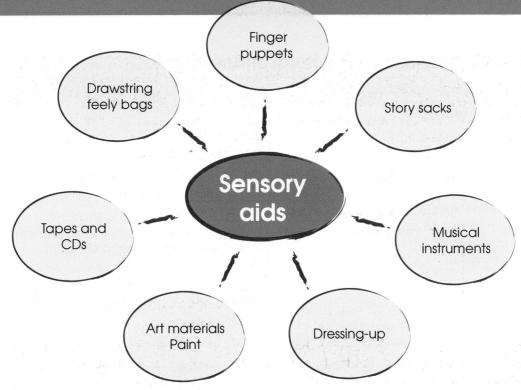

**Figure 1.3** Examples of sensory aids to support play and learning

Children might like to re-enact a story using dressing-up clothes and props in the role-play area. Children could use a story tape or CD to listen alone to a story they have enjoyed. They might create pictures they have seen or imagined from the book, drawing characters using paints and crayons. When investigating outdoors, children may come across objects or living things that they have read about.

Younger children enjoy hearing the same rhyme over and over again, and soon begin to join in with some of the words or actions.

**Task**

Look at Figure 1.3, which shows examples of sensory aids which can be used to support play and learning. Can you think of any other sensory aids that could be used?

**Task**

**In small groups:**

1 Choose a story that Stephanie, who is four and a half years old, and Jake, who is three years old, might enjoy.

2 Draw a spider diagram of all the sensory aids which would support the children's enjoyment and learning.

**Assessment task 2** ✓

Look back at Table 1.2. Copy one story from the table and then add one story of your own. Remember to include the sensory aid (equipment) you could use, and how you can encourage children to take part.

# Exploring the natural environment

## Important words

**Curiosity** – interest that is shown to learn new things or gain knowledge.

**Natural environment** – green spaces which may be planted with trees, contain rivers or are used as parks.

There are many learning opportunities for children when investigating and exploring the natural world. There are many places that adults can take children to learn about the natural environment and to develop the children's curiosity. Children are naturally curious, so it is very important to think about keeping them safe and out of danger when we take them out on visits.

Some children have lots of opportunities to explore the local environment, but children who live in crowded cities may not have open spaces near to where they live.

Being very curious, children will often pick up and explore objects that they find in the natural environment. Again, it is important that the adult makes sure that these objects are safe for children to touch.

Investigating and handling objects are very good way to learn about the environment. Children can examine objects such as shells and pine cones by using all of their senses. Some children may only have ever seen these objects before in books or on television. See Figure 1.5, which shows a child at the seaside. Some of the things a child may learn here are:

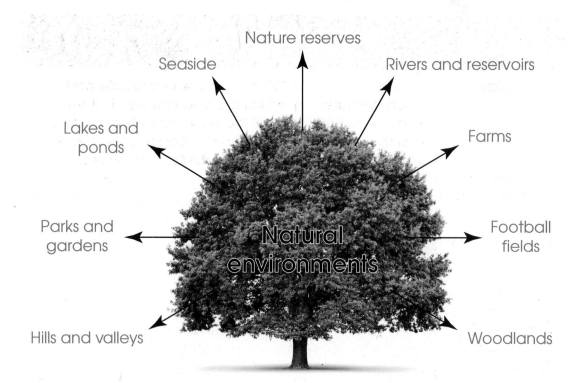

Nature reserves

Seaside

Rivers and reservoirs

Lakes and ponds

Farms

Parks and gardens

Natural environments

Football fields

Hills and valleys

Woodlands

**Figure 1.4** Examples of natural environments for children to explore

- what lives in rock pools
- what shells look and feel like and what creature lived in them
- how the sand feels under their feet
- how the texture of the sand changes nearer to the sea shore
- what the seaweed looks and smells like
- what the sea sounds like.

**Figure 1.5** There are many new things to learn at the seaside

### Assessment task 3 ✓

In small groups, discuss a natural environment in your area.

Copy Table 1.3 and fill in the empty boxes. Add another natural environment in the blank box and fill in the boxes about objects of interest and what children will learn.

### Important words

**Broaden children's experiences** – giving children the opportunity to take part in a wide range of activities or experiences, locally and within the wider environment.

| The natural environment | Objects of interest | What children can learn |
|---|---|---|
| The seaside | • shells<br>• sea creatures<br>• seaweed<br>• driftwood<br>• pebbles | What shells look and feel like and which sea creatures lived in them; what the seaweed looks and smells like; how driftwood and pebbles are shaped by the force of the sea. |
| In the woodland | | |
| In the local park | | |
| (in this box add another environment that you can think of) | | |

**Table 1.3** What children can learn from the natural world

## Community

There are many organisations, services and people who can help to provide experiences for children in the local area. The community can provide environments that allow children to try new things, learn skills and enjoy themselves.

Different services can give children the chance to widen their experience and learn new skills by providing them with activities to take part in. Some new experiences for them may be messy play sessions, gymnastics or music and song sessions.

---

### Examples of different community organisations

Sure Start

local children's centres

local library for books and toys

swimming clubs

toddler groups

tumble tots

dance classes

gymnastic clubs

rap and rhyme

indoor soft-play centres

adventure playgrounds

messy or sensory play workshops.

---

### Assessment task 4

List four services in the community. Discuss and write the two benefits for children of taking part in each of these four services. (For example, by taking part in a dance class, young children will learn about music and movement. They will be improving their gross motor skills and coordination. They may also may also make new friends and gain confidence.)

---

## Summary

Now that you have come to the end of this unit, you will have learnt that:

- children can learn in many ways, and use their senses to do this
- children enjoy investigating and finding out about the world they live in
- children enjoy stories and rhymes, and when encouraged by adults, children can learn lots of new things through books
- children are very interested in natural objects, and will enjoy looking at, feeling, smelling and listening to all kinds of natural objects when they are outdoors
- children might enjoy taking part in activities and services provided for them within their local community.

# Chapter 2

# CFC 14 Growth and development of young children

## What you will learn in this unit

You will gain an understanding of:

- the growth and development of children from birth to five years and 11 months
- different factors (issues) which affect growth and development
- the importance of a good diet and exercise for children's growth and development
- activities to support children's physical development
- ways to support children's language skills
- ways to encourage children to play socially (with other people and children).

## Growth and development

Babies and children not only grow bigger in size but also usually go through what are known as 'stages of development'. From birth, how babies look and what they can do change enormously.

- **Growth** is about the body growing and getting bigger in size and weight; for example, children grow taller and their feet get bigger. Growth happens naturally if children are healthy and well cared for.

- **Development** is about learning new skills, such as children learning to kick a ball or hop on one foot. Children need lots of different activities and the support of adults to develop new skills.

## Important words

**Milestones** – these are targets that children reach at certain points in their development; for example most babies can sit up by eight months.

**Milestones of development** tell us about the skills that children might have at a certain age. All children are different and grow at different rates. We must remember that not all children will follow these milestones; for example, some children learn to speak at a very young age, but might not be able to run and jump so soon.

## Factors that can affect children's growth and development

### Diet

A good, well-balanced diet will help to support children's healthy growth and development.

A poor diet might mean that children are not getting all the vitamins and nutrients they need to keep their body healthy. They may also have too much salt, fat or sugar in their diet, which could cause health problems.

### Exercise

Exercise gives children the chance to use their muscles to become strong, flexible and healthy.

Not enough exercise might cause children's muscles to become weak. They may build up too much body fat and become ill later in life.

**Figure 2.1** Growth and development can be measured

### Illness

Illness can affect a child's growth and development. Some illnesses can mean that a child may stop growing or grows very slowly.

Illness affects a child's development as they may spend time in hospital or be unable to go to school and play with their friends. They may not be able to learn new things or develop new skills.

### Disability or impairment

Disability or impairment may affect a child's development if the child is not given the correct support from adults. For example, a child who needs glasses (visually impaired) might not be able to see pictures in a book or the computer screen clearly.

However, if a child using a wheelchair is given the correct support, he or she should be able to enjoy most activities with other children.

## Lifestyle

The lifestyle of the child and family can have a good or bad effect on the child's development. If adults smoke in the house, close to where the child is sleeping or playing, the child could develop breathing difficulties.

> ### Important words
>
> **Patterns or stages of development** – when a baby or child develops a skill and then can move on to develop another more difficult skill. For example, the next stage of development for a baby who can stand will be to walk while holding onto an adult's hand.

# The stages of development of children from birth to six years

| Babies from birth to three months | | | | |
|---|---|---|---|---|
| **Physical development** | **Intellectual development** | **Language development** | **Emotional development** | **Social development** |
| Sleeps for around 18 hours each day.<br><br>Feeds every two to three hours during the day and will need to be fed less often during the night. | Begins to use senses to hear, smell and see what is going on around. | At first a baby is only able to cry, but quickly learns to make cooing and gurgling sounds.<br><br>Babies are soothed by the sound of familiar voices. | A baby will cry when in pain, hungry or uncomfortable, such as when they have a wet nappy or feel too hot or cold. | A new baby will try and look at faces, especially when they are being fed. By the age of three months a baby may copy an adult's smile. |
| **Babies aged three to six months** | | | | |
| **Physical development** | **Intellectual development** | **Language development** | **Emotional development** | **Social development** |
| Feeds three to five times every day. The baby can control head and arm movements, such as grasping a toy or rolling over on a play mat. | Greater development of senses: a baby will turn towards a sound, and learn who different people are by listening to their voice or looking at their face. | A baby at this age will make many different sounds, such as babbling and cooing when they are enjoying a bath, or grunting and crying when they are unhappy or tired. | Enjoys being cuddled and rocked. | Knows the difference between family members. Usually enjoys contact with family members, such as when feeding and being bathed. |

**Table 2.1** Developmental stages from birth to six years

| Babies aged six to 12 months (one year) | | | | |
| --- | --- | --- | --- | --- |
| **Physical development** | **Intellectual development** | **Language development** | **Emotional development** | **Social development** |
| Eats three meals and two snacks every day. Sleeps for around 12 hours every night and may have two naps every day.<br><br>Begins to control the body and hands by moving objects or pulling things towards them. At around eight months, a baby will begin to sit without support, and may start to crawl. | Enjoys playing: moves toys and objects from one place to another so that by the time the baby is 12 months old, they are able to stack one brick onto another. Babies enjoy looking at bright colours. | Babies easily recognise the people around them by the sound of their voice, and enjoy listening to songs and rhymes.<br><br>By 12 months a baby might say one or two words, and copy some sounds. | Babies may become clingy to family members because they are now more aware of strangers. | Gives and takes objects or toys.<br><br>May wave bye-bye.<br><br>By 12 months babies have learned to look when someone calls their name, and might understand some simple requests. |
| Children aged one to two years | | | | |
| **Physical development** | **Intellectual development** | **Language development** | **Emotional development** | **Social development** |
| Stands without support and begins to walk. Can climb up stairs, so needs to be watched! By the age of two years a child can run, throw and kick a ball. | Begins to make lines on paper with crayons or paints.<br><br>By the age of two years a child may enjoy building a tower of two bricks and pushing them over. | Children begin to repeat a few words and understand some instructions, such as 'coat on', 'come here'.<br><br>Understands about 50 words at two years of age. | A child may be interested in looking at themselves in the mirror, such as when clapping or pulling faces. | Enjoys simple clapping games such as pat-a-cake.<br><br>Enjoys feeding themselves. |

| Children aged two to three years | | | | |
| --- | --- | --- | --- | --- |
| **Physical development** | **Intellectual development** | **Language development** | **Emotional development** | **Social development** |
| Learns to jump off a low step, and may ride a tricycle.

Uses a spoon and fork properly when feeding themselves.

May take an interest in using the toilet or potty. | Uses crayons to draw in circular movements and make simple shapes.

Children may enjoy dough and messy activities.

They can also build higher towers by balancing more bricks.

Enjoys listening to others count and may begin to join in. | A child will put three or four more words together to make sentences: for example, 'me do that mummy' or 'little dog barking'.

Children will learn lots of new words and enjoy looking at picture books and listening to stories.

Understands over 600 words by the age of three years. | A child may be worried when family members leave them; the child may cry when starting nursery or if the parent goes out for the evening, leaving the child with a babysitter.

Understands the meaning of different facial expressions; for example, children will know when a person is happy or sad. | Uses 'I', 'me' and 'you'.

Copies actions, such as when singing rhymes at nursery.

Copies adults' actions by pretending to clean the car or stir food in a pan.

Can dislike sharing with others. Children at this age may enjoy playing next to other children but may not play with them.

Enjoys routines: a child may look forward to getting up and going to nursery every morning, or sharing a bedtime story each evening. |

| Children aged three to four years | | | | |
|---|---|---|---|---|
| **Physical development** | **Intellectual development** | **Language development** | **Emotional development** | **Social development** |
| Stands on one leg, jumps up and down.<br><br>Enjoys climbing and can change direction quickly when running in the play area. May now be able to take responsibility for their own toileting. | Draws circles with more control and may add lines for arms and legs or dots for eyes.<br><br>Can count up to ten and begins to learn the names of colours and shapes. | Understands over 1,000 words and makes sentences of four or five words.<br><br>Children now enjoy listening to longer stories and will often choose the same story over and over again. | Shows a sense of humour: may tell jokes and make funny faces or do silly walks.<br><br>Likes to spend time playing alone but also enjoys playing with other children.<br><br>May enjoy hugs and cuddles with family and friends. | Gives orders.<br><br>Enjoys playing with other children and will leave the main carer more easily, such as when going to nursery. |
| Children aged four to five years 11 months | | | | |
| **Physical development** | **Intellectual development** | **Language development** | **Emotional development** | **Social development** |
| Can open and close fastenings: can dress and undress for a PE lesson.<br><br>Can use scissors to cut out shapes and pictures.<br><br>Skips with a rope.<br><br>Runs quickly and safely around the playground without bumping into other children.<br><br>Is able to use a variety of large equipment such as swings and slides. Can throw a football and can sometimes catch it. | Can copy letters and numbers and can write their own name.<br><br>Draws pictures of trees, houses, people and animals.<br><br>Can complete a 20-piece jigsaw puzzle. | Children at this age know up to 2,000 words and use proper sentences. Children often talk clearly and will enjoy telling stories about themselves. | Enjoys caring for pets.<br><br>Shows concern when a friend is hurt.<br><br>Children will like to make choices for themselves, such as deciding which clothes to wear or what book to look at. | Children are now more able to do things for themselves, such as wiping up spilled juice.<br><br>They may also like to help other children, such as helping a younger child to complete a jigsaw.<br><br>Children at this age usually enjoy being busy and playing cooperatively. This means that they can agree rules of a game and take turns. |

## Supporting the growth and development of young children

As long as children are given food and water and their basic care needs are met, their bodies will grow taller and heavier.

However, in order for children to develop physically, they need more than food and water. Children need to be involved in activities which are suitable for their age and stage of development. They also need toys and equipment to play with, such as tricycles and scooters, or bricks and plastic cups to stack. Adults can provide the appropriate equipment and also make sure that the children are enjoying the activity and are safe and well supervised.

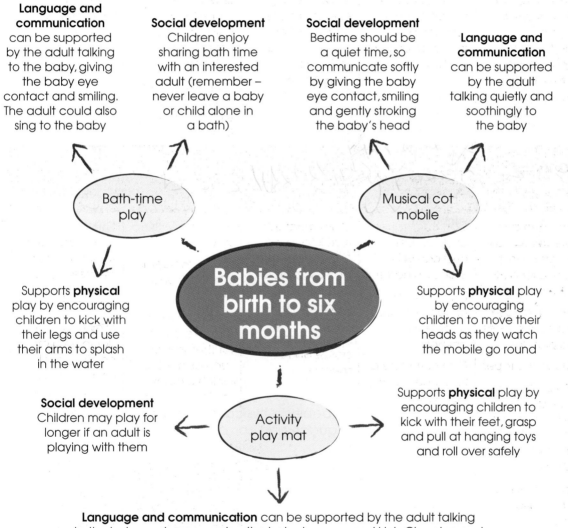

**Language and communication** can be supported by the adult talking to the baby, giving the baby eye contact and smiling. The adult could also sing to the baby

**Social development** Children enjoy sharing bath time with an interested adult (remember – never leave a baby or child alone in a bath)

**Social development** Bedtime should be a quiet time, so communicate softly by giving the baby eye contact, smiling and gently stroking the baby's head

**Language and communication** can be supported by the adult talking quietly and soothingly to the baby

Bath-time play

Musical cot mobile

Supports **physical** play by encouraging children to kick with their legs and use their arms to splash in the water

**Babies from birth to six months**

Supports **physical** play by encouraging children to move their heads as they watch the mobile go round

**Social development** Children may play for longer if an adult is playing with them

Activity play mat

Supports **physical** play by encouraging children to kick with their feet, grasp and pull at hanging toys and roll over safely

**Language and communication** can be supported by the adult talking to the baby and encouraging the baby to move and kick. Clapping and saying 'clever girl' or 'clever boy' will also encourage communication

**Figure 2.2** How activities support babies' physical development, social and emotional development and language and communication skills, from birth to six months

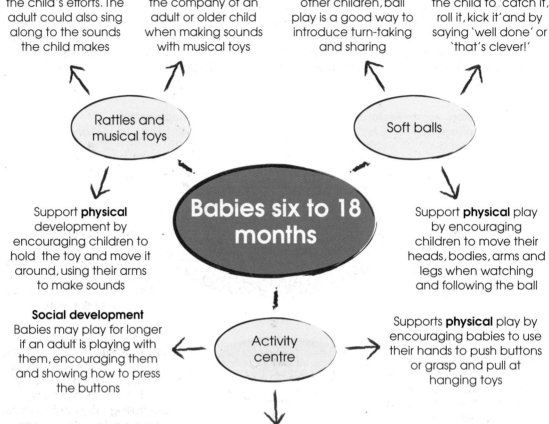

**Language and communication** can be supported by the adult encouraging the child through talking and praising the child's efforts. The adult could also sing along to the sounds the child makes

**Social development** Babies and young children will enjoy the company of an adult or older child when making sounds with musical toys

**Social development** When the child is with other children, ball play is a good way to introduce turn-taking and sharing

**Language and communication** can be supported by the adult giving encouragement to the child to 'catch it, roll it, kick it' and by saying 'well done' or 'that's clever!'

Rattles and musical toys

Soft balls

Babies six to 18 months

Support **physical** development by encouraging children to hold the toy and move it around, using their arms to make sounds

Support **physical** play by encouraging children to move their heads, bodies, arms and legs when watching and following the ball

**Social development** Babies may play for longer if an adult is playing with them, encouraging them and showing how to press the buttons

Activity centre

Supports **physical** play by encouraging babies to use their hands to push buttons or grasp and pull at hanging toys

**Language and communication** can be supported by the adult talking to the baby and using words such as 'push, pull, press', encouraging them by saying 'you do it'. Clapping and saying 'clever girl' or 'clever boy' will also encourage communication

**Figure 2.3** How activities support babies' physical development, social and emotional development and language and communication skills, from six to 18 months

## Task

In small groups, think about other activities for each of the age groups. Write down how they might support a child's physical development, social and emotional development, and language and communication skills.

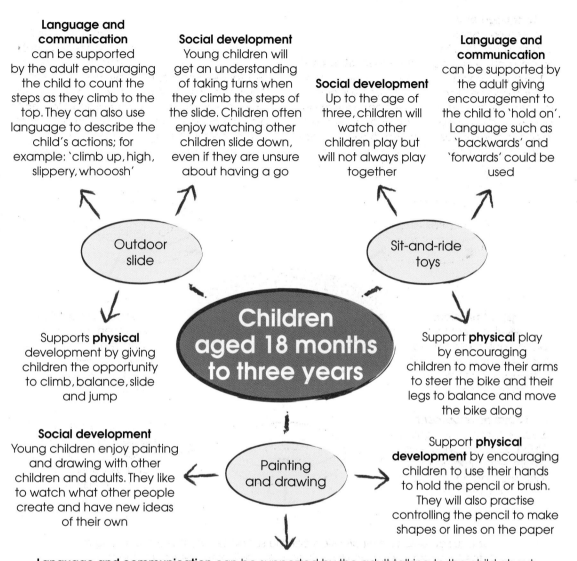

**Language and communication** can be supported by the adult encouraging the child to count the steps as they climb to the top. They can also use language to describe the child's actions; for example: 'climb up, high, slippery, whooosh'

**Social development** Young children will get an understanding of taking turns when they climb the steps of the slide. Children often enjoy watching other children slide down, even if they are unsure about having a go

**Social development** Up to the age of three, children will watch other children play but will not always play together

**Language and communication** can be supported by the adult giving encouragement to the child to 'hold on'. Language such as 'backwards' and 'forwards' could be used

Outdoor slide

Sit-and-ride toys

**Children aged 18 months to three years**

Supports **physical** development by giving children the opportunity to climb, balance, slide and jump

Support **physical** play by encouraging children to move their arms to steer the bike and their legs to balance and move the bike along

**Social development** Young children enjoy painting and drawing with other children and adults. They like to watch what other people create and have new ideas of their own

Painting and drawing

Support **physical development** by encouraging children to use their hands to hold the pencil or brush. They will also practise controlling the pencil to make shapes or lines on the paper

**Language and communication** can be supported by the adult talking to the child about what they are drawing or painting. This could be about the shapes they are making, the colours they are using and the way in which paints mix together on the paper

**Figure 2.4** How activities support babies' physical development, social and emotional development and language and communication skills, from 18 months to three years

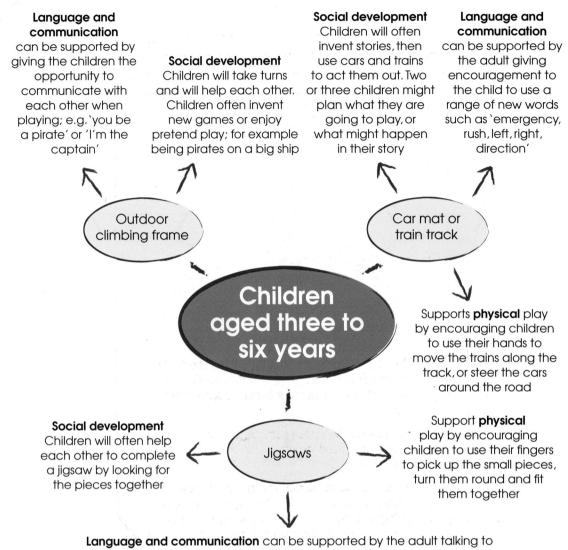

**Language and communication** can be supported by giving the children the opportunity to communicate with each other when playing; e.g. 'you be a pirate' or 'I'm the captain'

**Social development** Children will take turns and will help each other. Children often invent new games or enjoy pretend play; for example being pirates on a big ship

**Social development** Children will often invent stories, then use cars and trains to act them out. Two or three children might plan what they are going to play, or what might happen in their story

**Language and communication** can be supported by the adult giving encouragement to the child to use a range of new words such as 'emergency, rush, left, right, direction'

Outdoor climbing frame

Car mat or train track

**Children aged three to six years**

Supports **physical** play by encouraging children to use their hands to move the trains along the track, or steer the cars around the road

**Social development** Children will often help each other to complete a jigsaw by looking for the pieces together

Jigsaws

Support **physical** play by encouraging children to use their fingers to pick up the small pieces, turn them round and fit them together

**Language and communication** can be supported by the adult talking to the child about the picture on the jigsaw

**Figure 2.5** How activities support babies' physical development, social and emotional development and language and communication skills, from three to six years

## Assessment task ✓

Using some of the ideas in Figures 2.2, 2.3, 2.4 or 2.5, make one information card for each of these age groups:

- six to 18 months
- 18 months to three years
- three to six years.

Look at the information card shown in Figure 2.6, for a child aged 0–6 months. Make sure that your three activity cards give ideas for supporting the growth and development of young children, as in this example.

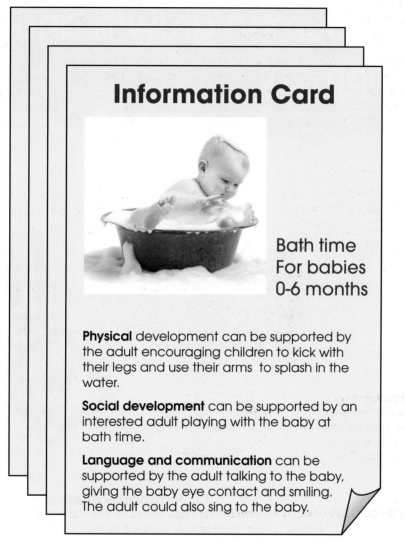

**Information Card**

Bath time
For babies
0-6 months

**Physical** development can be supported by the adult encouraging children to kick with their legs and use their arms to splash in the water.

**Social development** can be supported by an interested adult playing with the baby at bath time.

**Language and communication** can be supported by the adult talking to the baby, giving the baby eye contact and smiling. The adult could also sing to the baby.

**Figure 2.6** Sample information card

## Summary

Now that you have come to the end of this unit, you will have learnt about:

- the stages of children's growth and development from birth to five years 11 months
- the factors (issues) that affect growth and development, such as diet and exercise
- different activities which can support children's growth and development.

# Chapter 3

# CFC 15 Human growth and development

## What you will learn in this unit

You will gain an understanding of:

- stages of growth and development that people go through
- factors that may affect physical growth and development
- effects of ageing later on in life.

### Important words

**Wellbeing** – health.

**Emotional and social wellbeing** – happiness in yourself and as part of a group (society).

### Case study

Grace is 82 years old. She lives alone because her husband died two years ago. Grace has lived an active life but has recently suffered a stroke. She has made some good progress, and as she is getting better, she is hoping to leave the hospital soon to go home.

Grace's daughter lives nearby, so she will help Grace by making her dinner and doing jobs around the house.

Before Grace is allowed to leave the hospital, a specialist nurse must assess how well Grace will be able to manage at home. She needs to find out about Grace's physical, intellectual, emotional and social wellbeing.

Grace enjoyed swimming all her life, and swam twice a week in the local pool as a child and throughout her life until she reached 74 years of age. Grace always made sure that she ate a good balanced diet, but during her teenage years she did admit to smoking for a couple of years. However, she realised it was unhealthy and soon stopped smoking.

She caught measles when she was seven years old, which made her very ill. Grace had slight hearing loss in one ear because of this illness.

The happiest times in Grace's life were when she married Bob, her husband, and when her children were born. The time when Grace was most sad was when her husband died; she then had to live alone. Another difficult time for Grace was when she suffered the stroke. This made her very frightened and worried about how she would look after herself in the future.

# Human growth and development 1.1

People move through different stages of growth and development during their lives. When we are talking about a person's lifetime, we can look at five important 'life stages', which are shown in Figure 3.1.

| Infancy | Childhood | Adolescence | Adulthood | Adolescence | Childhood | Infancy |

**Figure 3.1** A timeline of different life stages

## Infancy

This is the time between birth and five years. It is a time when young children need their families to provide everything they need, as they are not able to care for themselves yet. Although some children at this age will not be at school, they are still learning at a very fast rate. During this time children change from being a tiny baby to a school-aged child who can walk, talk and begin to care for themselves.

### Childhood

This is the time in a child's life when they start full-time school and begin to have their own friends. The stage of childhood begins at the age of five, and continues until a child is about 12 years old. Again, growth and development are happening quickly and a child changes very much during this stage.

### Adolescence

This stage in a person's life begins at around 12 or 13 years of age, as they become a teenager. During this teenage stage, the body goes through many physical changes which are linked to reproduction (having babies). Hormone changes inside the body can affect growth, mood and appearance. Some teenagers find this stage of their life quite difficult, but most of their worries will have disappeared as they reach adulthood.

### Adulthood

When people move into adulthood, they probably have a job, a partner and perhaps even a family of their own to care for. Physical growth and development have stopped, and later in adulthood the body begins to show signs of ageing; for example, a person may not be able to run so fast or climb so many stairs. However, social and emotional changes are still happening at this time and the brain is still working very well.

### Older adulthood 2.3

During this life stage people are more likely to become ill or physically less able. This is because a person's body is beginning to wear out, particularly if they did not take care of their bodies when they were teenagers and adults. If we smoke or drink too much alcohol, it could damage our bodies.

During this life stage, skin begins to lose elasticity so will become lined; hair will lose its colour so become grey. Muscles weaken, so walking may become slower and tasks such as taking tight lids off jars may be difficult.

Some older people might have sight or hearing loss. Many older people live alone due to the death of a partner, so may become lonely. Getting out and meeting friends can become more difficult if people are worried about going out alone or when it is dark.

## Task

In small groups, think about an older person that you know (it could be a neighbour or grandparent). Discuss the effects that ageing has had on this person.

**Figure 3.2** Older adulthood brings many challenges

### Assessment task 1

**Make a poster showing:**

- a pathway of Grace's life. Remember to include all five stages: use pictures from magazines or draw what a person at each stage will look like.

- a brief description of the effects of ageing that Grace may have experienced during older adulthood.

- what is meant by physical, intellectual, emotional and social development. Use the information below to help you.

### Important words

**Pathway** – a timeline.

# What are physical, intellectual, emotional and social development? 1.2

### Physical development

This means the way in which bodies grow and how people develop physical skills. As we move into older adulthood, physical skills or activities may become more difficult. A baby learns to walk, a child learns how to run and jump, a teenager might run quickly and jump over objects, a adult might run even faster; however, as people become much older this might become more difficult. As they age, some older adults may need a stick to support them when walking.

## Intellectual development

This is the way in which our brain develops and works. As we go through the different life stages, our brain takes in more information that we can understand and use. However, as we move through older adulthood, the brain may start to slow down and we may become forgetful or confused.

## Emotional development

This is the development of lots of emotions, from sad to happy and excited to angry. During each stage people have different emotions to deal with.

### Example!

A teenager may worry about exams or friendships, whereas an adult may worry about household bills or the family.

## Social development

This is about understanding the needs of others as well as your own, within social relationships. It is about understanding how to behave in different places; for example, children need to understand how to behave towards teachers and their friends in school, and teenagers have different social experiences in college. Older adults might lose partners or friends, and need to find new ways to socialise.

## Factors affecting growth and development 2.1

As a person goes through the life stages from birth to older adulthood, there are many factors which may affect physical growth, such as exercise, diet, lifestyle or illness. (See Chapter 15, Healthy Living (HL 1) for more information about factors affecting growth and development.)

### Important words

**Factors** – negative or positive things that may have happened.

**Circumstances or life events** – situations or experiences in a person's life.

### Life events which can affect emotional and social wellbeing 2.2

There are also certain times in a person's life that can affect their emotional and social wellbeing. Good experiences that make an adult feel happy may include a birth in the family, getting married, getting a good job or moving to a nice house. There could also be times in an adult's life when they feel sad or very worried, such as losing a home or a job, a family splitting up or the death of a close family member.

## Task

Think about different events or factors that have affected your physical health and experiences and your emotional and social wellbeing.

**Figure 3.3** A wedding is an important life event

## Assessment task 2

Using what you have learnt about Grace:

1. list three factors that may have affected her physical health and development during her lifetime.

2. list three experiences in Grace's life which may have affected her emotional and social wellbeing.

## Summary

Now that you have come to the end of this unit, you will have learnt that:
- there are five main life stages
- factors such as diet, lifestyle and exercise can affect physical growth and development
- events such as the birth of a child or the death of a close family member are called 'life events'
- life events can affect a person's social and emotional wellbeing.

# Chapter 4

# CFC 9 Respecting and valuing children

## What you will learn in this unit

You will gain an understanding of:

- how to respect and value children as individuals
- why it is important to value children as individuals
- ways to respect and value children
- the rights of children.

## How to respect and value children as individuals 1.1

Every baby, child, teenager and adult is different. Children are all individual and they may have very different lifestyles. A child may live with just their dad, or there may be three or four children at home with their mum and their grandparents. Some children may live in a caravan within a community of travellers; others may spend time with foster carers if there is a difficulty in the family, such as a parent or primary carer who has to go into hospital. Children are all very different, but every child has the right to grow up feeling happy and loved.

### Important words

**Self-image** – this is about your feelings and thoughts about yourself.

## Task

Look at the pictures of the four friends in Figure 4.1. They are all very different. In small groups, write down some of the things that make them individual.

Some of the things that make the children individual could be:

- the colour of their skin
- the type of food they eat
- how the children are expected to behave at home
- religious beliefs
- what the children enjoy doing.

## Why adults should value and respect children 1.2

It is very important for all adults to treat everyone with respect, as children look at the way in which adults behave and copy their behaviour.

**Figure 4.1** We all have individual appearances

### Example!

If adults talk kindly to children and listen to what they say, the children will feel important and will learn that it is good to listen to others.

### Important words

**Respecting children** – this is when you feel and behave positively towards children.

| Ways in which adults can value children as individuals | Reasons why this is important for children |
|---|---|
| Understand what each child enjoys doing and provide activities around these interests | This will make children feel that they are understood and included. They will feel that their interests are valued. |
| Allow children to speak and listen to what they say | This will make children feel that they are important enough to be listened to. This will make them feel respected. |
| Speak kindly to children | This will give children the confidence to talk to adults and share their feelings. Children copy the way in which adults speak to others. |

**Table 4.1** How and why adults should value children

| Ways in which adults can value children as individuals | Reasons why this is important for children |
|---|---|
| Understand that all children have different learning needs | Meeting children's individual learning needs helps them to develop and learn at their own pace. This will help them to feel valued. |
| Give all children the support and encouragement they need to play and learn | This will give children the confidence to try new things and feel proud of themselves. |
| Be good role models by learning about different cultures | The adult can encourage children to take an interest in cultures and lifestyles that are different from their own. This will make all children feel valued. |
| Respect children's different cultures and lifestyles | This will make children feel that their culture and lifestyle are important. |

### Important words

**Lifestyle** – the ways in which a person lives their life and the choices which they make.

**Personality** – how a person thinks and behaves.

### Assessment task 1

1. Draw a spider diagram showing all the ways in which adults can value children as individuals, using Table 4.1 to help you.

2. Think about a young child who attends nursery or school. Think about their personality and their likes and needs. Why would it be important for adults to respect this child as an individual?

## How to make children feel respected and valued 2.1

The way in which an adult behaves towards a child is very important. If we show children kindness and give them our time, they will understand that they are important and valued. One way to show children that we respect and value them is through communication.

### Communicating with children to ensure that they feel valued

Communication can be verbal and non-verbal. Verbal communication is when people use sounds, words and sentences to talk to each other. Non-verbal communication means other ways of communicating such as eye contact, facial expressions and body language (bear in mind, however, that eye contact is not always an appropriate form of communication within some cultures).

It is very important that adults communicate with children in ways that help them feel valued and respected. Some ways to communicate well with children include the following suggestions:

- **Smile when meeting the child** – this will show you are pleased to see them.

- **Give good eye contact if appropriate** when a child is speaking – this will show them that you are interested and listening to them.

- **Stand near to a child, but not too close** – this will respect their need for space.

**Figure 4.2** It is important to engage with children

- **Get down to the child's level** – this will make the child feel comfortable and show them that you care enough about what they have to say.

- **Use positive language**, such as 'well done' or 'tell me about your picture' – this will show the child that you are interested, and they will feel valued.

- **Always listen carefully** to what the child is telling you – this helps a child to feel that you respect what they have to say.

- **Take time to answer a child's questions** – this will show the child that you have time for them and are interested in how they feel.

## Appropriate adult behaviour
## towards children 2.2

It is important that adults know how to behave in front of children, because children learn by copying what they see and hear. If children see adults treating others with respect, they will learn that this is the right way to behave. It is therefore important that adults are polite, friendly and show children respect, as this will help to make the children feel secure and valued.

It is very important that all adults encourage children to respect each other, so that they feel valued, happy and included as they grow up.

### Important words

**Facial expression** – these are the faces we make that others use to understand what we mean.

### Task

Think about how people treat you in school, college, in the supermarket or in your neighbourhood.

- How do they behave towards you?
- How does this make you feel?
- How do you behave towards them?
- How could you behave in a more positive way?

Adults should support the child's learning to understand that everyone is an individual. This includes neighbours, friends, shopkeepers and teachers at school. Differences between children should be seen as positive things that make each child special. If children know that it is a good thing to be different, they may feel good about themselves and respect differences in others.

Other ways to show children that they are valued and respected are shown in Figure 4.3.

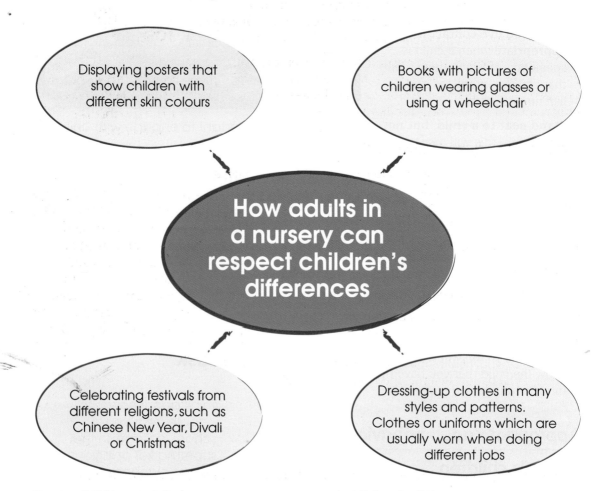

**Figure 4.3** How adults in a nursery can respect children's differences

**Assessment task 2**

1. Write down three ways to communicate with children and say why these ways will make them feel valued (use the list on the previous page to help you).

2. Write down three ways of behaving towards children to show that you respect and value them (look at some of the examples in the spider diagram to help you).

## Children have rights 3.1

### Laws and organisations which support children's rights

Decisions about how a country is run are usually made by the government. Members of the government make rules which everyone should follow, called laws. Many laws exist to support children's rights, and there are many organisations who care about the lives of children. They provide services to support children and promote their rights. Some organisations are in the local area where you live, whereas others are based in larger cities.

A person is chosen by the government to focus on the lives and rights of children, who is given the title of 'Minister for Children.' This Minister understands that children are important and have rights, just like adults.

### What are the rights of the child?

Adults who work with children should understand 'The Rights of the Child', which the United Nations Convention on the Rights of the Child promotes for all children in the world. These include the right to:

- feel happy and secure
- be protected from harm
- be listened to and valued
- a health service (doctors, hospitals)
- an education.

All of these rights help to make sure children are valued and grow up to be happy, healthy and responsible adults.

### Task

In pairs, list some of the rights that you think all children should have.

### Assessment task 3 ✓

Look on the internet or in books to find out about the organisations and people that support the rights of the child. Write down or print off the information that you find.

---

## Summary

Now that you have come to the end of this unit, you will have learnt that:

- all children must be respected and valued as individuals by the adults around them
- there are many ways to communicate with children to make sure they feel valued and respected
- adults should behave in ways that show children respect
- laws are made to make sure that the rights of children are understood by adults
- there are many organisations that support the rights of the child.

# Chapter 5

# CFC 10 Children's play and leisure activities in the community

## What you will learn in this unit

You will gain an understanding of:

- play and leisure activities for children in the community
- ways in which children's development can be supported through play and leisure activities
- the role of the adult in supporting all children during play and leisure activities.

## What are play and leisure?

All children have an equal right to relax and play safely, both on their own and in groups. Children should have the chance to take part in activities that will interest them and help to keep them fit and healthy.

Play is something that interests all children and it is important for their development. It is so important that the government has made laws to try and make sure that all children have the chance to play safely in their community.

### Example!

There are centres which provide children with activities after school and during the school holidays. These activity sessions allow children to play safely while their parents may be at work.

### Task

Write down a list of places where you could enjoy indoor or outdoor activities in your local area.

# Play and leisure activities for children in the local community

**1.1** **1.2**

There are many different kinds of organisation which provide different play and leisure activities within a local community.

## Important words

**Leisure activities** – activities or hobbies that children might enjoy.

**Local community** – the places and people near to where we live.

**Figure 5.1** Swimming is a popular leisure activity and sport

## The local council

Local councils provide many different activities for children within the local community. These might include activities in leisure or sports centres, swimming pools, playgrounds and parks. Schools and Early Years Centres often provide after-school clubs and holiday activity sessions.

## Voluntary groups

Voluntary groups are usually organised by people who meet to help and support each other and their families. An example of a support group is a group of parents or carers of children with particular needs or a disability, meeting to share experiences and to give their children opportunities to play together. Another example is a group of parents or primary carers running a toddler group together.

**Figure 5.2** Children enjoy belonging to different groups

Voluntary groups include Brownie and Cub/Scout groups, that children can join and enjoy activities, learn new skills and sometimes take part in camps and adventure holidays.

### Private play companies

Many private companies provide play opportunities for children, such as indoor soft-play centres or 'jungle'-style gyms that allow children to climb, jump and play together on the ropes, slides and in the ball-pool.

### Specialist teachers

Specialist teachers give children private lessons in activities such as music or dance. A specialist teacher could also be a sports coach who gives private football or rugby lessons.

### Local sports clubs

Sports clubs often run children's team games or practice sessions; for example, the local cricket club, rugby club or football club.

> ## Important words
>
> **Leisure facilities** – places which provide an opportunity to relax and enjoy activities.

**Figure 5.3** Belonging to a sports club can boost a child's fitness levels and social skills

## Churches and religious groups

Groups that have indoor church halls and outdoor gardens sometimes allow families and children to use their facilities. Play groups may be run in the halls, and summer fairs may be held in the gardens.

## The benefits of play

## activities for children (2.1)

Children can benefit in many ways from taking part in leisure and play activities. The activities can support physical development, social and emotional development and language and communication skills.

> ### Assessment task 1
>
> Produce a poster showing local play and leisure facilities for children.
>
> List four organisations that provide play activities for children, and give examples of what these activities could be.
>
> (You can use both indoor and outdoor activities for your examples.)

## Task

In pairs, discuss indoor or outdoor activities that you took part in when you were growing up. How did these activities support your physical development? Did you learn any new words? Which social skills did you need to use?

An example of these benefits can be seen in Table 5.1 below.

| Activity | Area of development | How children's development is being supported |
|---|---|---|
| Playing football at the local club | Physical | Running in straight lines and changing direction. Kicking and throwing the ball. |
| | Social and emotional | Team building, agreeing rules, learning to stay positive when the other team scores. Celebrating together when your team wins. |
| | Language and communication | Players shouting to each other to pass the ball. Learning new words for the different team positions. |

**Table 5.1** How different activities support children's learning

**Assessment task 2**

Produce a chart like the one above, showing the benefits of taking part in three indoor or outdoor activities.

# The role of adults in supporting play and leisure activities in the community 3.1

## How to support children in play and leisure activities

Children need adults to support them, in order to enjoy play and leisure activities. Adults can do this by getting involved in activities in the community such as volunteering to help out at school clubs or sports teams.

The role of the adult is to:

- make sure that all children can take part in activities suitable for their age and stage of development

- ensure that all the children are included and enjoying the activity

- support the children to understand the rules of behaviour and/or the rules of the game

**Figure 5.4** Some adult supervision is required for play and leisure activities

- support children to enjoy team games by organising them into teams or giving roles and responsibilities, such as deciding with the children which child will be goalkeeper first

- supervise all children to make sure they are playing safely. The adult may need to check the activity for risks and hazards before the children take part – this is called risk assessment.

- make sure that the equipment and resources are safe for everyone to use.

### Factors which might prevent (stop) children from taking part in leisure activities 3.2

There are sometimes reasons why families and their children find it difficult to take part in the play and leisure activities in their community. For example:

> **Important words**
>
> **Factors** – parts of a person's life which can affect them.

- **money** – the activities or equipment may be too expensive for some families, especially if they have quite a large family

- **distance** – a family might live in a rural area and find it difficult to travel on the buses to community centres in the local town

- **time of day** – some play and leisure activities may be early in the morning or in the afternoon when families are busy making dinner

- **the ages of the children in a family** – parents or carers may have very small children or babies and so will need space and activities for them to use as well as the older children

- **parents' and carers' time** – many parents have to work, so may not be able to take their children to the places where play and leisure activities are held. This could also be a problem if the children always need parental supervision

- **illness of a parent** – if a parent has an illness they may not be able to take their child to different play and leisure activities.

## Including children in play and leisure activities 3.3

Adults can make sure that all children are included in play and leisure activities. Extra thought and care might be needed if a child has a particular need or a disability.

Table 5.2 gives examples of some particular needs and disabilities and ways in which adults can include children.

**Figure 5.5** Children with disabilities should be included in play and leisure activities

| Particular need or disability | How adults can give support |
| --- | --- |
| Asthma: the child may need to be given rest and medication | Supervise the child to make sure that they are given a chair in which to rest. Read medication instructions and make sure medication is given by the responsible adult at the correct time. |
| Different language: some children may not speak or understand the language | Make sure that the child can join in activities by demonstrating how they are done. Find somebody who speaks the same language so that they can explain, or use a translator. |
| Age of child: a young child may be just beginning to use the potty or toilet | Ask the child if they need the toilet and make sure that they and their parents know where to find the nearest toilet. |
| A child may not see as well as other children, and need to wear glasses | Make sure that the child has clean glasses to see through, and that they do not become damaged during an activity. |
| A child may not hear as well as other children, and need to wear a hearing aid or grommets | Make sure that the child can hear and understand any instructions that are being given; speak slowly and clearly. |
| A child may use a wheelchair | Activities or equipment may need to be changed slightly so that the child can join in, such as the height of tables, ramps into the building or toilets. Adults may need to give one-to-one support to join in certain activities such as ball games. |

**Table 5.2** How adults can support children with different needs or disabilities

It is very important that all children are given the opportunity to take part in play and leisure activities in their local community.

Adults need to think about ways of supporting children so that they can take part, which could include finding out about bus routes or organising care for other children in the family. Remember that children with particular needs or disabilities may need some special equipment or different support from adults to help them to take part in an activity.

## Assessment task 3

1 Choose one of the following leisure activities:

- a swimming session for children of all ages, in the local swimming pool on Saturday mornings from 9 to 10 am: cost £2.00

- a dance class in the town hall, from 4.30 to 5.30 pm every Friday, for children aged four to eight years: cost £4.00.

2 Write down two factors which may stop a child from taking part in the chosen activity.

3 Write down ways in which adults can support all children to take part in this activity, including children with particular needs or disability. Use the table above to help you.

4 Write down two ways in which the swimming coach or dance teacher will support the children during this session.

## Summary

Now that you have come to the end of this unit, you should understand that:

- different local organisations provide play and leisure activities for children
- children can enjoy many different indoor and outdoor activities in their local community
- children's physical, social and emotional development and language skills can be supported through taking part in play and leisure activities
- some children may need extra support from adults to help them take part in play and leisure activities.

# Chapter 6

# CFC 16 Preparing for your next steps

## What you will learn in this unit

In this unit you will gain an understanding of:

- how to achieve your chosen career
- how to find out about training courses and jobs
- how you should describe your skills and experience in a CV
- how to apply for jobs and prepare for an interview.

## Investigate career goals 1.1

It is important that when you are making decisions about a future career, you have lots of information and advice to help you make choices. There are many different jobs in the childcare world, and also many different childcare courses that give you the qualifications you need to work with children.

### Important words

**Job** – something you spend time doing to earn money.

**Career** – jobs that take you in a certain direction, for example childcare or nursing.

**Career goals** – what you want to achieve from your career.

### Next steps 1.2

It is important to spend time thinking about what career goals you would like to achieve. When you have found a job or career that you are interested in, you need to look at the next steps to take in order to make this happen.

## Task

Use the internet or newspapers to find out about the different courses you could take, or childcare jobs you could apply for.

### Important words

**Training** – courses which help a person to gain qualifications.

There are usually a number of steps that need to be taken to reach a goal. Figure 6.1 shows the different steps to be taken by a person wanting to work with children.

It may be helpful to think about training courses or experience that you will need to gain a job in this area of interest.

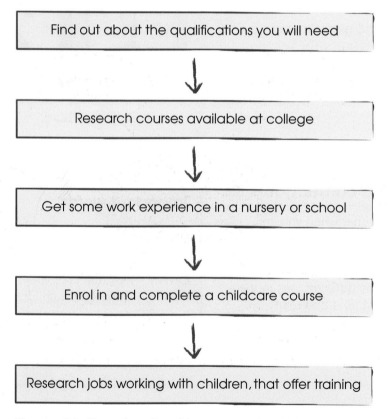

**Figure 6.1** Steps leading to a career in childcare

**Figure 6.2** Training, skills and job opportunities for childcare work

**Figure 6.3** There are many steps to take for a career in childcare

## Possible barriers to reaching career goals

There may be barriers that make it more difficult for the next steps to be taken, when you are trying to reach your career goals. It is important to think about how you can get around these barriers, so that they do not stop you from taking further steps on the path to your chosen career.

Figure 6.4 gives examples of possible barriers to reaching your career goals.

### Important words

**Barriers** – things that may get in the way of achievement.

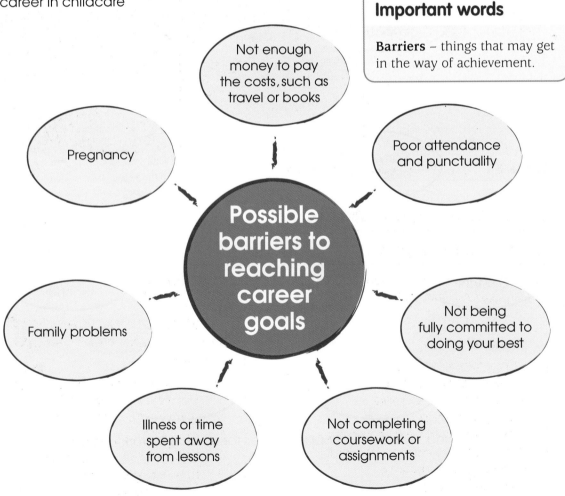

Not enough money to pay the costs, such as travel or books

Pregnancy

Poor attendance and punctuality

**Possible barriers to reaching career goals**

Family problems

Not being fully committed to doing your best

Illness or time spent away from lessons

Not completing coursework or assignments

**Figure 6.4** Possible barriers to reaching your career goals

## Assessment task 1

Using a table like the one below:

- write a list of your career goals or jobs that you would like to do
- write down the next steps that can be taken to reach the goals
- write down some of the problems or barriers that might stand in your way.

| My career goals | What do I need to do next (next steps)? | What might stop me from doing this? |
|---|---|---|
| | | |
| | | |
| | | |

**Table 6.1** Considering your career path

# Where to find information about
# training and employment 2.1 2.2 2.3

You can find information about training courses and job vacancies in a chosen career in many places.

**Example!**
- the internet
- the local newspaper
- national newspapers
- the job centre
- popular childcare magazines
- college information booklets
- through Connexions
- a career advisor

## Assessment task 2

In pairs:

- find information about training or jobs with children that you are interested in
- using this information, decide which steps you would need to take to get this job or go on this course.

# Outlining your personal skills 3.1

When you are going along a chosen career path and applying for training courses or jobs, it is important to think about your own skills and qualities, your interests and experiences.

## Important words

**Career path** – the direction a person takes their career in.

## Task

Copy Figure 6.5 and write down your:

- skills (what you can do well, for example being organised, good timekeeping, good team player, good communication)
- qualities (positive things that you can bring to a job, such as being helpful, patient and caring)
- interests and work experiences.

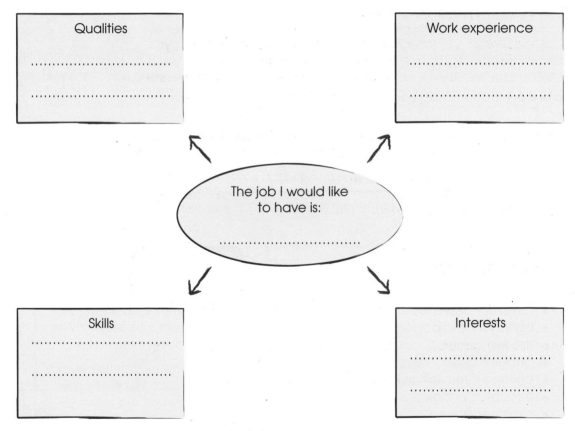

| Qualities |
| ......................... |
| ......................... |

| Work experience |
| ......................... |
| ......................... |

The job I would like to have is:

.........................

| Skills |
| ......................... |
| ......................... |

| Interests |
| ......................... |
| ......................... |

**Figure 6.5** Your qualifications for a job

## Filling in a CV 3.2 3.3

Often when you are applying for jobs, you are asked to fill in a CV. This is simply information that you need to provide to the person or company that has advertised the job. They use this information to choose the person most suitable for the job.

There is an example of a CV in Figure 6.6.

### Important words

**CV** – a list of your skills and knowledge.

### Assessment task 3

Use the example of a CV in Figure 6.6 on the next page to create your own CV. Think about all of the information that will be needed: a brief description of your qualifications, skills and experience which would relate to your identified career path. Also take time to include relevant personal information which may help you to get the job interview.

### Task

Look at the CV in Figure 6.6 in small groups. Do you think that this person shows that they have the skills and qualities to work with children?

## The recruitment process 4.1

Once you have seen a job advertisement that you are interested in, you will need to apply for the job. You need to ask for an application form to be emailed or posted to your home address. When you have filled out the application form or written a CV, you should post or email it back to the person or organisation who has advertised the job vacancy.

When the application has been looked at, you may be asked to go for an interview if your skills, qualities and experience match the needs of the job.

This process is known as the recruitment process. It starts when a job is advertised in a local newspaper or job centre and ends with somebody suitable getting the job and starting work.

### Important words

**Recruitment** – how a person with the right skills can be found and chosen for the right job.

**Recruitment process** – applying for a job, preparing and going for an interview.

**Corinne Victoria Ward**
17 Morley Street
Winterset
Wakefield
DX 19 9XZ
Telephone 01999 630323

I am a hard-working early years student studying on the CACHE level 1 childcare course. I try very hard to gain good grades, and when I finish the course in July 2011, I hope to achieve a good grade. I am organised and always hand my work in on time. I am polite and respectful to others and my college reports say that I am beginning to develop all the skills required to be a good childcare assistant. I am patient, kind and really enjoy looking after young children.

In my spare time I enjoy jogging and I have recently run in a half marathon. I had to plan my training for this race and train properly to make sure I was fit for the race. I think this shows that when I am focused on doing something, I can be successful. In my spare time I also enjoy babysitting my cousin who is four years old, and I would love to work with children.

**Qualifications**

| Subject | Level | Grade | School/college | Date |
|---|---|---|---|---|
| Food Hygiene | Certificate | Pass | Food Safety Limited | 2009 |
| English Language | GCSE | D | Winterset Common School | 2010 |
| Maths | GCSE | E | Winterset Common School | 2010 |
| Art | Level 1 | Pass | Winterset Common School | 2010 |
| First Aid | Certificate | Pass | Wakefield Central College | 2011 |
| CACHE level 1 childcare | Certificate | complete July 11 | Wakefield Central College | |

**Work experience/jobs**

| Place of work | Job title | Responsibilities | Date start–finish |
|---|---|---|---|
| Rob's Fish and Chips Street Side Rd | Catering assistant | Mainly responsible for serving customers and making sure that the serving area is kept clean at all times. After closing time I help to wash all the surfaces and floors. | Jan 09–present |

**Hobbies and interests**
I enjoy keeping fit by swimming and I go for a five-mile run every weekend. I enjoy being with my family and playing with my four-year-old cousin. I often go to the cinema with my friends at the weekend.

**References can be gained from**

Emma Barker
College Tutor
Wakefield Central College

Robert Fryer
Rob's Fish and Chips
Street Side Rd

**Figure 6.6** A sample CV

✓

## Assessment task 4a

It is important to understand the recruitment process so that you know what needs to be done when you are applying for a job.

In pairs, look at the steps below. Put into the correct order the steps you should take to secure a job.

- complete application form or CV
- accept the offer of an interview
- return application form
- accept job offer
- look for suitable job vacancies
- attend interview
- prepare for the interview

Even though you have applied for a job, you may not get it. It is important to keep trying, as usually many people apply for the same job.

## Preparing for an interview 4.2

The more prepared you are, the more chance you have of being successful. It is very important to prepare well before an interview. See Figure 6.8 on the next page.

## Assessment task 4b

Write down four reasons to be well prepared for an interview.

**Figure 6.7** You will feel much more confident at an interview if you have prepared well

**Figure 6.8** Good preparation for an interview

## Summary

Now that you have come to the end of the unit, you will have learnt that:

- you need to know which steps to take to reach your career goal
- barriers sometimes get in the way of taking next steps
- there are many opportunities for training and jobs, and you can find information in many places
- it is very important to prepare yourself when applying for jobs and training courses
- a CV contains information that could help you to get a job, and it is important to include all your skills and qualities that are needed for the job
- it is important to prepare well for an interview to make sure that you have a good chance of being successful.

# Chapter 7

# CFC 17 Supporting babies to play

## What you will learn in this unit

You will gain an understanding of

- ways of supporting babies' development through play
- the different play activities for babies (from birth to 15 months)
- the role of the adult when providing play activities for babies.

You will also learn about toys and activities suitable for babies from birth to 15 months.

## Supporting babies' development and needs through play 2.2

Play is sometimes called 'children's work' because it is something that most children and babies like to spend their time doing. When children and babies play they are having fun and will be learning lots of new things.

Play is a very important way to support babies' individual needs and development, because it gives them lots of opportunities to explore and try new things. Babies will spend time exploring objects with their senses. They need to be given activities that they are interested in, so that they do not become bored.

Babies use all of their muscles when they play, so play helps them to develop strong muscles as well as good hand-and-eye coordination and a sense of balance.

Babies can practise holding and moving toys: for example, a baby shaking a rattle will learn about how to make sound by holding and moving an object. A baby may learn the names and sounds of farm animals when playing with a toy farm.

Figures 7.1, 7.2 and 7.3 show ways in which to support babies' physical, intellectual and emotional development.

> **Important words**
>
> **Physical development** – when our bodies grow and we are able to develop new skills; for example, running and jumping and then riding a bike.

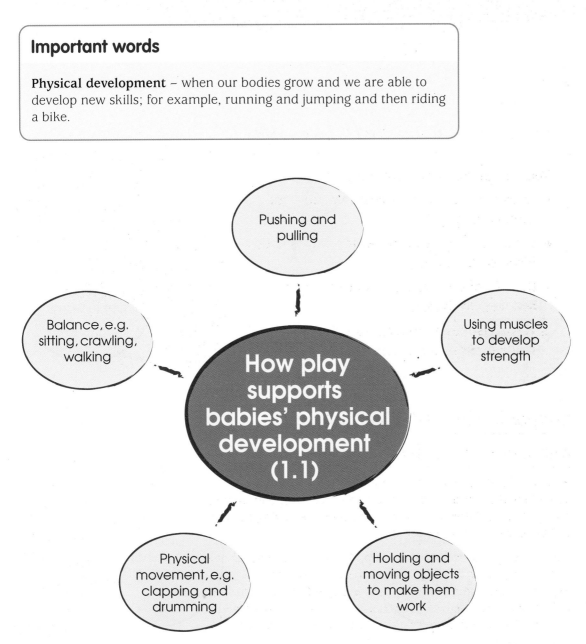

**Figure 7.1** How play supports babies' physical development

## Important words

**Intellectual development** – when our brain develops and we begin to understand more; for example, children learn to read and write.

**Language development** – this starts when a baby is born and begins to communicate by crying. The baby hears sounds and begins to copy what they have heard. This is the beginning of language development.

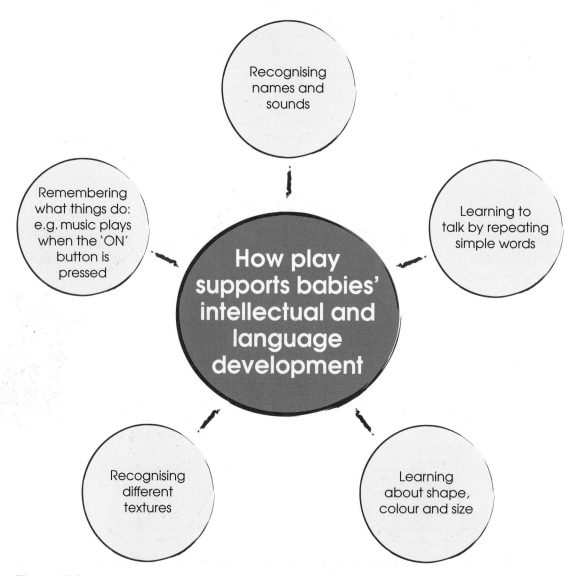

**Figure 7.2** How play supports babies' intellectual and language development

## Important words

**Emotional development** – the development of many different feelings, from sad to happy and excited to angry.

**Social development** – understanding the needs of others as well as your own, and understanding how to behave in different places.

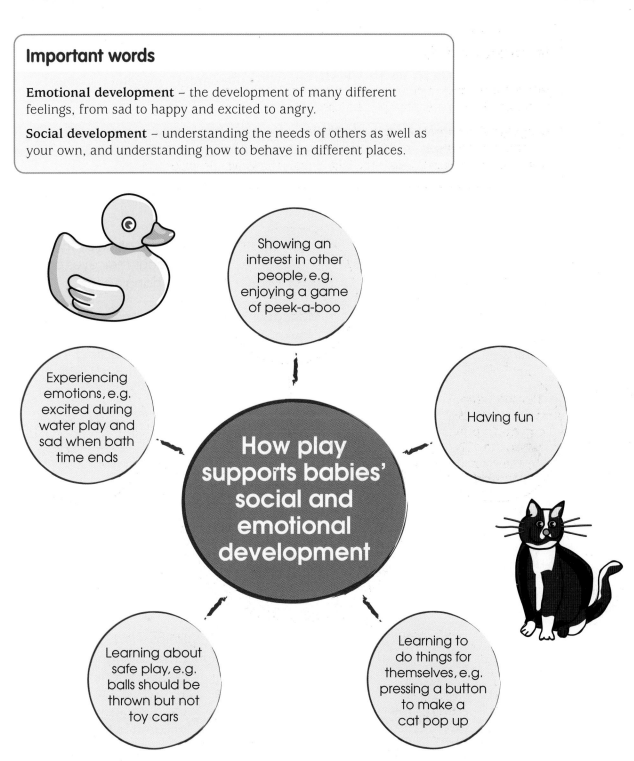

**Figure 7.3** How play supports babies' social and emotional development

# The different play activities for babies (from birth to 15 months)

**Important words**

Resources – toys and equipment.

| Age | Activity | Resources | Benefits for the baby |
|---|---|---|---|
| Birth to three months | Listening to music | Musical toys | Music can soothe a crying baby. |
| | Watching moving objects | Mobiles | Babies will enjoy trying to focus their eyes on the hanging toy. |
| Three to seven months | Exploring, kicking and rolling | Musical animal play mat | Physical movement to reach and touch the animals; hearing the sounds the animals make. |
| | Bath-time play | Floating fish | Grasping the fish in the water helps to develop physical skills. |
| Seven to 12 months | Building towers and knocking them over | Soft cubes | Learning how to build a tower and enjoying watching it fall. |
| | Hand painting | Paints and paper | Enjoy feeling the textures and looking at the patterns in the paint. |
| 12–15 months | First steps | Push-along trolley | Helps with balance and physical strength and development. |
| | Story time | Glove puppets | Encourages young children to talk and concentrate on the puppet. |

**Table 7.1** Benefits of different toys and resources for a baby

## Choosing safe and suitable toys for babies 3.1

It is the job (role) of the adult to choose toys that are suitable for the age of the baby. If babies are given toys that are too difficult for them to use, they will not enjoy playing with them and may become upset or cross.

### Toy safety

Some toys may have very small parts; this would make them unsafe for babies and young children. Adults must make sure that the toys which babies and young children play with are safe. All toys sold in the UK should display a symbol which shows the safety and quality of the toy. Table 7.2 shows the different safety symbols used on toys, games and clothes.

| Symbol | What does it mean? |
|---|---|
| **0-3** (no under-threes logo) | This logo means that the toy is not suitable for children under the age of three years. The under-threes put everything into their mouths to explore shape and texture. If they are given toys which have small parts, younger children could swallow or choke on them. Toys with this sign should not be given to children under three years. |
| Lion mark | The Lion mark is a safety mark which shows that the toy is safe and also of good quality. If you buy a toy with this label, you can be sure that it has passed all the safety tests. |
| Kite mark | A toy or product can only show this Kite mark when it has passed all the tests and meets all the high British safety standards. The Kite mark is the symbol that promises customers that this toy is safe and reliable. |
| CE | The CE mark on a toy label means that the toy meets all of the safety standards required by European law. |
| BEAB Approved | The BEAB Approved mark is an electrical safety mark found on electrical items used in the home, including children's equipment. This symbol means that the equipment has been made correctly and is safe to use. |

**Table 7.2** Symbols on children's equipment, clothing and toys

### Age-appropriate toys

Some companies selling toys write messages on the package to help you choose a suitable toy; for example, it might state 'recommended for children aged three to four years'.

Age guidelines can help you choose the right toy for the baby or young child. For example, a ten-piece jigsaw is too difficult for babies aged 11 months, so they would not enjoy or learn from this activity.

## Task

Using a catalogue or pictures from the internet, make a collage showing a collection of toys suitable for these age groups:

- birth to six months
- six to 12 months
- 12–18 months.

Remember the safety marks! A toy that is not suitable for children under the age of three years should not be chosen for these age groups.

## The role of the adult when providing play activities

## and supporting babies during play activities 3.2

Babies and young children are individuals; they learn in different ways and are interested by different things. When providing toys and activities for children, adults should think about their ages and interests. By choosing toys and equipment which are suitable for the baby's age and ability, you are supporting the baby to have fun and learn through play.

Below are some guidelines for providing and supporting play activities.

- Provide suitable clothing for messy play.

- Check that equipment such as paintbrushes and crayons are suitable for the baby's age.

- Provide toys which could help the baby to learn new skills.

- Make sure that the play area is safe and there are no dangers; for example, cables and plug sockets.

- Check that there is enough space for the baby to be able to move around safely.

- Observe the baby to make sure that they are safe and enjoying the activity.

- Show the baby that you are interested by smiling and using supportive language; for example, 'you do it', 'clever boy'.

- Support the baby to explore the toy to find out how it works or what it does.

- Remember that the baby needs time to find out for themselves – do not take over the baby's play.

- Support the baby when they need it; for example, show the baby how the toy works if they are struggling.

- Make sure that the area is inviting by using bright toys and perhaps soft music.

## Task

In pairs, choose three toys for babies aged from birth to 15 months. State what age the toy is suitable for, and why these toys could be good to support a baby's development.

**Figure 7.4** An adult can support a baby's development through play

| The age of the child | The activity, toy and resources that might be used | The area of development being supported | The role of the adult in supporting individual needs |
|---|---|---|---|
| Birth to three months | Hanging a musical toy on the baby's pram | | Choosing toys that are suitable by checking the symbols and recommended age. Always watching to make sure that the baby is safe. Removing the toy when the baby has had enough or is too tired. |
| Three to seven months | Placing the baby onto a colourful play mat | | Always watching to make sure that the baby is safe. Making sure that there are no dangers around the mat such as plug sockets or toys that the child could roll onto. Understanding when the child has had enough. |
| Seven to 12 months | | Social and emotional development | |
| 12–15 months | Making pictures using coloured play foam on paper. Resources: <br> • coloured foam <br> • plastic bowls <br> • large sheets of paper | | |

**Table 7.3** How activities and adults support learning through play

## Assessment task 1

Copy Table 7.3, which explores the role of the adult in supporting babies's development and needs through different activities. Fill in the blank boxes with your own examples.

## Assessment task 2

Design a poster showing what adults need to do to keep babies safe during play.

On the poster, include five ways that adults can encourage babies to play. (Read pages 60 and 61 for guidelines about playing with children.)

## Summary

In this unit you will have learnt that:

- play is good for babies' development
- safety is very important when babies are enjoying play.

# Chapter 8

# CFC 21 Science activities for young children

## What you will learn in this unit

In this unit you will gain an understanding of:

- science activities suitable for children aged from 18 months to five years
- how to set up science activities to support children's learning
- possible health and safety risks when doing science activities
- what children can learn from doing science activities.

## Science activities suitable for young children 1.1

Children of all ages enjoy experimenting and investigating the world around them. They like to find out about how things work and what they do.

Children use their senses to discover new things: see Figure 8.1.

### Example!

By using all of their senses, children have the opportunity to find out about the world around them.

**Figure 8.1** Using senses to explore the world

Often adults do not pay attention to things that happen around them in everyday life; they are so used to seeing them that they do not think about them. However, often these will be new experiences for children.

**Example!**
- watching fairy cakes rising in the oven
- seeing how boiling water makes steam
- watching spring flowers pushing up through the earth
- hearing the leaves crunch under their feet in autumn
- feeling ice cream melting in their hands on a hot day
- touching wet clothes as they dry on the line
- tasting new foods and experiencing how they feel on the tongue

## Task

Look around you (and perhaps out of the window!). Can you see anything that could be called science happening around you?

## Important words

**Resources** – the equipment and tools needed for an activity.

**Health and safety risks** – things or situations that could be dangerous and cause harm.

**Figure 8.2** Children can enjoy learning about science through play

# Setting up science activities to support young children's learning

## Resources

These are the equipment or tools that will be needed for the activity. You will need to prepare these before the activity begins.

## Health and safety

When planning science activities for children, it is always important to think about everyone's health and safety.

### Example!

If you are baking with children and using the oven or a hot surface, it is important to keep children safe and explain the dangers to them. Sharp equipment should always be kept out of the reach of young children.

### Assessment task 1

Look at the table of science activities below. Complete the table to show how you would prepare a washing-and-drying activity for children aged from 18 months to two years, and a floating and sinking activity for children aged three to five years.

| Age of child | Science activity | Description of the activity | Resources needed | Health and safety |
|---|---|---|---|---|
| 18 months to two years | Wet sand play | Adding water gradually to sand tray, so that children can feel how the texture of the sand changes as the water is added. | sand tray<br><br>sand<br><br>plastic jug<br><br>water<br><br>aprons (to keep child dry) | Spilled water should be mopped up so that no one slips.<br><br>Children should be supervised closely so that they do not throw sand or put it in their mouths. |
| 18 months to two years | Ice cube water play | Put ice cubes into a bowl of warm water and allow the children to feel the ice melting and watch the cubes become smaller and disappear as they melt. | plastic bowl<br><br>warm water<br><br>ice cubes (frozen in advance)<br><br>aprons | Mop up water spills.<br><br>Supervise child to make sure they do not put ice cubes into their mouths (as they could choke).<br><br>Make sure the water is only warm and not too hot. |
| 18 months to two years | Washing dolls' clothes and hanging them up to dry | | | |
| Three to five years | Planting a sunflower seed and watching it grow | Children plant a seed in a plastic plant pot filled with compost. Children water the seed regularly.<br><br>Children will see the plant begin to grow, and see the leaves and petals open. | plastic plant pot and saucer (stops the water leaking onto the floor)<br><br>sunflower seeds<br><br>compost and a small watering can | Close supervision to make sure that seeds are not put into children's mouths and compost is not eaten or thrown.<br><br>Mop up water spills.<br><br>Wash hands after touching compost. |

| Three to five years | Making chocolate crispy cakes | Melt chocolate in a bowl over a pan of hot water. Add cornflakes or crispies and stir well until the chocolate covers all the cornflakes. Put bun cases into a bun tin. Spoon the mixture into bun cases and allow to cool in the fridge. | pan of hot water bowl wooden spoon chocolate bars corn flakes or crispies bun cases bun tin fridge | Make sure that everyone washes hands before starting the activity. Make sure children do not burn themselves on the pan of hot water: explain the dangers to the children. Remove the pan away from the children once the chocolate has melted. Do not leave the children alone with the hot water. Clear up any spills of water. |
| Three to five years | Finding out about floating and sinking in the water tray | | | |

**Table 8.1** Some suitable science activities to do with children

## Supporting children who are carrying out science activities  2.2

Science activities support children's understanding of the world around them, how things work and what things do. Children playing with cars on a mat will be discovering about pushing and pulling, and how things move.

Adults need to understand that sometimes children need space and time to find things out for themselves. If the child playing with the cars on a mat is enjoying moving the cars around, an adult should watch and not interrupt. However, if the child becomes bored, the adult could give the child a ramp to see if the car moves faster.

At other times the child may need support to carry out the activity. This could be because it involves a danger such as heat, or it could be because the child does not really understand how to do something, such as how to make cakes or buns.

**Figure 8.3** Children need careful supervision for some science activities

Adults should:

- support children by making sure that they have the correct resources available to carry out the science activity

- always think about health and safety, and keep children safe while doing the activity

- think about ways to support children to learn new things while enjoying the activity.

<br>

**Assessment task 2** ✔

Look back at the science activities you have completed in task 1.

1. Draw a spider diagram to show what the children could learn from each activity.

2. Write down what kind of support the children may need from adults during each activity (remember that this will include resources, health and safety and supporting children to understand).

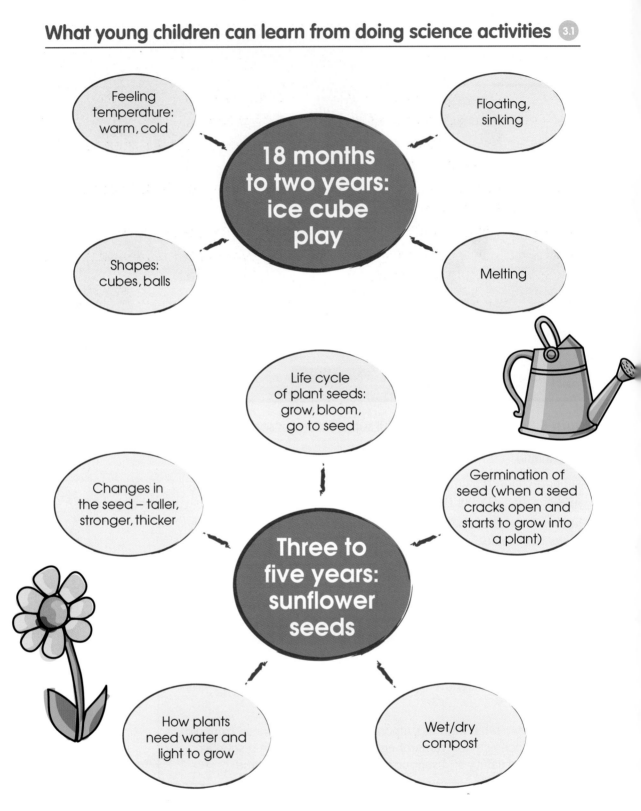

**Figure 8.4** What young children can learn from doing science activities

## Summary

Now that you have come to the end of this unit, you will have learnt that:

- many science activities are suitable for young children
- adults need to think carefully about setting up science activities and the resources that may be needed
- adults should always make sure that children are safe by thinking about their health and safety
- children will need different types of support to enjoy the activities
- young children can learn lots of new things from science activities when adults support their learning.

# Chapter 9

# CFC 22 Technology activities for young children

## What you will learn in this unit

In this unit you will gain a greater understanding of:

- technology toys and activities that are suitable for young children
- how technology toys and activities can help to support children's learning and development.

## Technology toys or activities suitable for children 1.1

There are many different technology toys available to buy for children. Toy designers are always trying to design new electronic toys and games that will help children to develop and learn.

Many of the electronic toys and games that have been made for children had to be used when the child was sitting down or being still. This meant that some children were not getting much exercise when they were playing with the toys, which was seen as a bad thing. Technology toys are now being designed so that children need to move around to use them; for example, sports games on a computer console need children to move in order to play them.

### Important words

**Electronic toys** – toys and games that need power to work, usually from electricity or batteries.

**Technology toys** – toys which usually have some kind of simple computer built in.

**Figure 9.1** Some technology toys can be used from birth

## Babies from birth to one year

A range of technology toys is available for babies, such as electronic books, soft animals that make sounds and electronic activity mats. Popular technology toys for babies include educational activities on bouncers and baby gyms where babies can touch buttons to make light and sound.

## Toddlers aged one to two years

When children reach the toddler stage, there are many different technology toys that they can enjoy.

**Example!**

- pretend phones that make sounds
- story readers
- play computers that help children to learn the names of objects or learn colours
- electronic dolls that make sounds
- push-along walker toys

## Children aged three to five years

There are even more educational technology toys for this age range. Computers have programs which teach children shapes, numbers, letters and colours. Child-friendly digital cameras are popular for this age group.

There are computer games machines that work with the television, which can give children the chance to be active while they are learning.

## Task

Look at the activity centre in Figure 9.2. When children press the buttons, the name of the picture is sounded.

- Think of a topic that children might be interested in.
- Use a computer to design your own activity centre, adding picture buttons for children to press (draw the activity centre if you do not have access to a computer). Write down what the children will do.
- Think of other actions that could be added into your activity centre, such as flashing lights or music.

**Figure 9.2** An activity centre

## Benefits for the child of using technology toys 1.2 2.1

There are many benefits for children of using technology toys:

- Children can learn the rules of an activity and also how to take turns; for example, a bowling game on a games console teaches children to take turns, to count and to develop control of the hand-held remote control.

- Children learn that it is all right for them to make mistakes, and that if they try again they will get better at the activity with practice.

- Benefits to physical development include helping a child to learn how to control their bodies or improve their balance.

- Benefits to intellectual and language development could include learning the names of colours, learning how to count, and learning new words or how to copy sounds.

**Figure 9.3** Using digital cameras can be fun for young children

## How technology toys can support children's learning 2.2

As we have seen above, technology toys can help children learn many things and boost their physical, intellectual and language development.

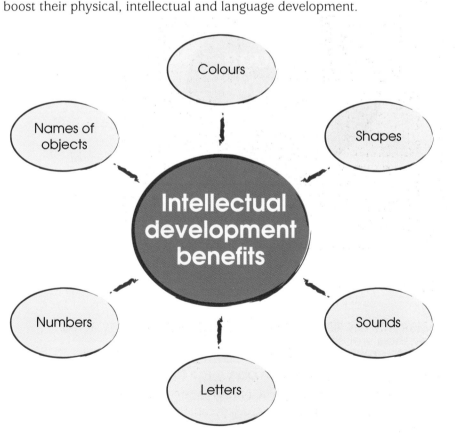

Colours

Names of objects

Shapes

Intellectual development benefits

Numbers

Sounds

Letters

**Figure 9.4** How technology toys can support children's learning

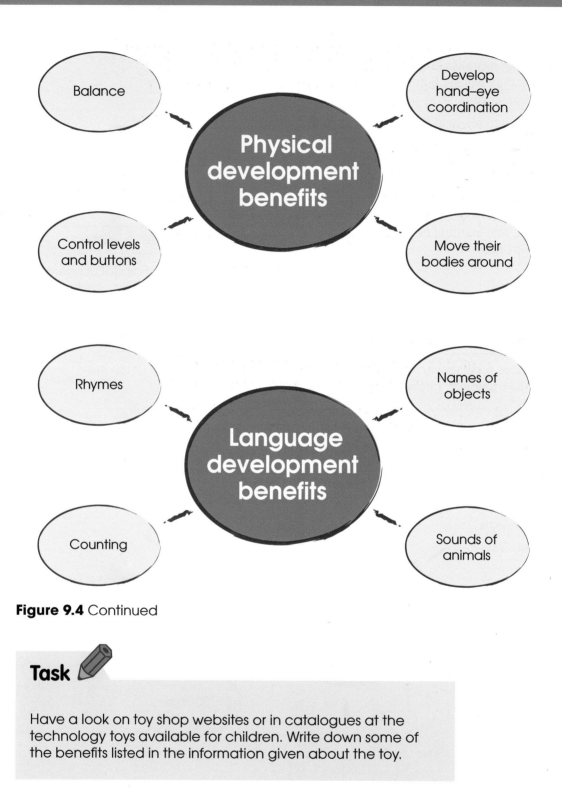

**Figure 9.4** Continued

## Task 🖊

Have a look on toy shop websites or in catalogues at the technology toys available for children. Write down some of the benefits listed in the information given about the toy.

## Assessment task

1. Make a poster using pictures of nine technology toys cut out from magazines or catalogues:

    - three toys for children from birth to 12 months old
    - three toys for children aged from one to two years
    - three toys for children aged from three to five years.

2. Write down the physical, intellectual and language benefits for children when they use the toy you have chosen.

## Summary

In this unit you have learnt that:

- young children can enjoy many technology toys and activities which can help them to learn while being active
- technology toys and activities can support children's physical skills, and their intellectual and language development.

# Chapter 10

# CFC 23 Musical activities for young children

## What you will learn in this unit

In this unit you will gain an understanding of:

- the benefits of musical activities for young children (aged from three months to five years)
- how to plan musical activities
- how to make safe musical instruments for young children
- what young children can learn from musical activities.

## Musical activities for young children 1.1 1.2

Most people enjoy listening to music. Some people enjoy playing instruments to make their own music, while others prefer to dance or exercise to music. Most people have a favourite type of music, such as classical music, dance, rap or one of the many other types of music. Some people listen to music to relax or to try and change their mood. Others find it easier to concentrate when they are listening to music, such as when doing homework.

### Important words

**Musical instruments** – objects which make musical sounds.

Children also enjoy listening to and making sounds. These sounds can be called music if they have some kind of rhythm or beat.

Babies might feel soothed by soft music playing, and will often show they are enjoying the sounds of the music by stopping crying or turning their heads to show they are listening, or by using their arms and legs to move

**Figure 10.1** Playing with musical instruments is a popular activity for children

to the sounds they can hear. Adults can give babies opportunities to enjoy music by singing to them, playing musical CDs or giving them musical toys such as jingle bells, musical cot mobiles or soft toys that play a tune.

It is important that the music is not played too loudly as young babies have very sensitive hearing that can easily be damaged. Loud noises could also scare young children.

**Figure 10.2** Babies sometimes find music soothing

### Important words

**Sensitive hearing** – when someone is aware of very small sounds.

## Task

Use catalogues and magazines to cut out pictures of musical toys and equipment for babies and young children.

- What age of child is the toy or instrument suitable for?
- What can children do with the toy or instrument?

**Assessment task 1** ✓

Complete Table 10.1 to show what the children could enjoy and learn from each musical activity.

| Age of child | Suitable activity or musical toy | What the children could enjoy and learn |
| --- | --- | --- |
| Baby from three to 12 months | Cot mobile | The child might enjoy listening to the sounds and watching the mobile move. |
| | Soft musical toy | Young children quickly learn that a certain toy makes a sound, and will enjoy listening to the sound. You can buy toys with a gentle rhythm that sounds just like a heartbeat, which can help to soothe a distressed baby. |
| | Soft music played from a CD | Even very young babies might feel comforted and soothed by the sound of soft music being played. |
| 12 months to 2½ years | Musical activity centre<br>Drums and pans | |
| 2½ to five years | Making a shaker<br>Singing along to familiar music and songs | |

**Table 10.1** Musical activities suitable for young children

## Making musical instruments and games 2.1 2.2 2.3

Children enjoy experimenting with the sounds that different instruments make. They will be excited about making and using their own instrument.

### Instruments which children can make

There are many different instruments that adults can make with young children. Some examples are given here.

**Sandpaper blocks**

These are two small blocks or bricks which are both covered on one side with coarse sandpaper. The blocks are rubbed together to make a 'rasping' sound.

**Musical triangle**

Wire coat hangers are bent into a triangle shape. The hook of the coat hanger is bent down so that string can be threaded through for the child to hold. A metal spoon can be used to 'ting' on the side of the triangle.

**Ice-cream tub drums**

Empty ice-cream tubs can be decorated and used as drums. Wooden spoons can be used as drumsticks.

**Task**

Look at the examples above and then use the internet, books or magazines to find out about other instruments that are suitable to be made by young children.

**Figure 10.3** Plastic bottles can also be used to make instruments

81

## Musical activities and games

Children often enjoy activities and games where music is used. Music is often used within activities to encourage children to dance or move. Children might enjoy games such as 'musical chairs' or 'musical statues', in which music is played and suddenly turned off; children then have to find and sit on a chair or stand very still.

Some children's television programmes use music or songs to encourage children to sing, copy actions or join in with dance moves.

### Assessment task 2

Choose one of the above ideas for making an instrument or think up an idea of your own, and plan the activity. Use the sample activity plan in Table 10.2 to help you.

| Activity plan to make a musical shaker | |
|---|---|
| Age of children Numbers of children | • Two to five years<br>• Children aged two years will do the activity on their own with the adult. Older children will be in groups of three. |
| Resources | • Plastic bottles with tightly fitting lids<br>• Strong sticky tape<br>• Dried beans, small dried pasta shapes, rice or sand (to make sounds in the bottles) |
| What the children will do | 1 Children will carefully wash out the containers and dry completely with a cloth or towel.<br>2 Children will tip a small amount of one of the dry products into the bottle and screw on the lid tightly.<br>3 The strong sticky tape should be wrapped around the lid to make sure it cannot be taken off. |
| What children will learn | • Children will enjoy making the rattle.<br>• Children will enjoy shaking the bottle to make sounds. Different dry products will make different sounds, so children will enjoy experimenting with how different sounds are made.<br>• Children will also enjoy listening to a music tape and shaking out the rhythm. |
| Health and safety | • The adult must check that all the bottles are undamaged and that there are no sharp edges.<br>• It is very important that the adults watch children closely when they handle the dry products to make sure that they do not put them into their mouths.<br>• Adults should make sure that the lids are very tight, so that they do not fly off when the bottle is shaken. |

**Table 10.2** Sample activity plan

## Summary

Now that you have come to the end of the unit, you will have learnt that:

- there are many musical activities that young children can learn from and enjoy
- there are lots of different instruments that adults can make with young children
- activity plans help you to think about the skills that children could learn when doing the activity, and what the adult can do to make sure that the activity is enjoyable and safe.

# Chapter 11

# CFC 24 Practical health and safety when with young children

## What you will learn in this unit

You will gain a greater understanding of the following:

- the meanings of symbols and instructions on young children's equipment and toys
- health and safety instructions
- health and safety rules, guidelines and instructions when taking children out of the setting
- health and safety equipment and safety features
- potential hazards to young children in the home
- how to make sure that young children stay safe in the home
- safety equipment and controls which help to keep young children safe outside the setting
- possible fire hazards to young children and adults in a house.

### Important words

**Potential hazard** – a possible problem or danger.

**Fire hazard** – something that may cause a fire.

## Health and safety guidelines and instructions

### Children's equipment and toys 1.1

All toys and equipment given to children should be checked to make sure that they are both safe and suitable for the age of the child. Checking toys for damage such as cracks or loose parts will help to keep children safe when playing.

There are many safety symbols to look for when choosing safe and suitable toys. Look back at Table 7.1 in Chapter 7, Supporting babies to play (CFC 17) for information on the different safety symbols and logos.

## Task

Make a booklet called 'Health and safety for children'. Use this booklet to complete all the assessment tasks in this unit.

### Important words

**Health and safety guidelines/ guidance** – information about how to stay healthy and safe.

**Health and safety symbols** – signs or stamps used to show that something is safe to use.

**Health and safety instructions** – rules that are given to follow to keep people safe.

### Assessment task 1

Look at safety labels and instructions on toys and equipment. In your booklet, draw the symbols that you find on three items, and write down what you learn from the label or the instructions.

## Safe use of household cleaning products and chemicals 1.2 2.1

Household cleaning products and chemicals can be very dangerous. All containers have warnings if they could cause harm, and instructions telling you what to do in an emergency. If some chemicals come into contact with your skin or are swallowed, they can make you very ill or could even kill you.

**Figure 11.1** Cleaning products should be kept away from children

### Important words

**Cleaning products** – liquid or powders used to clean floors, cookers or carpets.

It is important to keep all cleaning products away from children, and if possible store these products in a locked cupboard. Here are some very important safety points to remember:

- Read the labels of the products you use in your home and the setting.

- Look for these words on bottles and packages: 'Caution', 'Warning', 'Poison', 'Danger' or 'Keep out of reach of children'.

- Keep these products in a safe place, locked away from children.

- Put the lid back on straight after using the product.

- Do not pour cleaning products into other containers such as a juice bottle, because someone else, especially a child, might think that it is safe to drink.

- Some cleaning products can give off dangerous chemicals if they are mixed with other products; for example, if bleach and vinegar-based products are mixed together, a dangerous chlorine gas is given off.

Figure 11.2 shows examples of the symbols on the side of cleaning products.

**Figure 11.2** Safety symbols which are shown on cleaning products

### Assessment task 2

Look at the label on a household cleaning product. In your booklet, write down the name of the product and copy the important information from the label. Figure 11.3 gives an example.

| Warnings | Danger: Harmful if swallowed. This product contains sodium hydroxide. Wear long rubber gloves when using to avoid it touching the skin. Avoid contact with all skin, eyes, mucous membranes (mouth, lips/nose) and clothing. |
|---|---|
| **Severe health effects:** | From inhalation (breathing in) this product. Causes burns on contact. Eye contact: Causes burns to eyes on contact. Skin contact: causes burns to skin on contact. Ingestion: harmful if swallowed. May cause burns to mouth, throat and stomach. |
| **First Aid:** | • If this product splashes in EYES: immediately rinse eyes with water and continue rinsing eyes for 15 minutes. Call a doctor if necessary. <br>• If this product touches the SKIN: rinse skin immediately and remove clothing that has the product on. Wash thoroughly with soap and water and continue rinsing with water for ten minutes. If the skin is damaged, see a doctor. <br>• If you breathe in the fumes from this product, known as INHALATION: move person to fresh air. Call a doctor if the person is at all unwell. <br>• If you swallow this product, known as INGESTION: DO NOT make the person sick. Rinse mouth thoroughly with water, drink water or milk. Call a doctor immediately. |

**Figure 11.3** A sample cleaning product label

## Outdoor safety for children 1.3

There are many dangers in the world around us. It is very important to think about these dangers when taking children outdoors.

Water hazards – children should always be closely watched when they are anywhere near water, so that there is no danger of children drowning.

Dogs and dog toilet areas – adults should look out for soiled areas, and never allow children to touch dogs or other animals that do not belong to them.

Roads and traffic – always make sure that adults help children to cross the road safely. Teaching children about road safety is important.

Litter (broken glass, needles, sharp objects) –adults should safely remove any sharp or dangerous objects, and never allow children to pick up or touch any litter that is sharp or dangerous.

Poisonous plants – adults should be aware of any harmful plants and remove them if possible. Children should not touch or taste any seeds, berries or leaves.

Uneven surfaces and slopes – children should be reminded to walk carefully, looking where they are walking.

# Hazards in the home 2.1 2.2

Although we might think that our homes are safe places for children, every year many children are seriously injured or die because of accidents in the home.

Most of the accidents that happen to children in the home can be avoided. Adults need to take care to keep children safe in the home by supervising them carefully and never leaving them alone if there is a chance that a child could be harmed.

Being tidy and organised can help to keep children safe. Adults are more likely to spot hazards if the house is well organised. Table 11.1 includes some household hazards and safety equipment needed to create a safe place for children.

## Important words

**Safety features** – a part of something that makes it safe to use, such as seatbelts in a car.

**Safety equipment** – equipment that keeps adults and children safe, such as car seats or fire blankets.

**Safety controls** – things that can be done to keep safe.

| Hazard/task | Risk to the child | Safety equipment needed and ways to reduce the chance of children being injured or becoming seriously ill |
|---|---|---|
| Trailing wires and cables | Tripping up or getting the cord round their neck and being strangled | Keep wires and cables tidy and away from children.<br>**Use a cable tidy** (which is cheap to buy).<br>Never have cables trailing across the floor. |
| Plug sockets | Child could poke items or fingers into the socket, receiving a serious electric shock which could cause death | When the sockets are not being used, cover them with a **socket safety cover**. |
| Bath time | Drowning in the water; being scalded by very hot water; serious burns could cause scarring or even death to a child | NEVER leave children alone at bath time even for a minute; they should always be supervised.<br>Always put the cold water into the bath first so that if the child climbs in before you have checked the temperature, they are less likely to be scalded.<br>Use a **thermometer** to check the temperature – which should be between 37°C and 38°C. |

| Hazard/task | Risk to the child | Safety equipment needed and ways to reduce the chance of children being injured or becoming seriously ill |
| --- | --- | --- |
| Sleep time | Suffocation or falling out of bed | Babies and young children should always sleep in a cot so that they do not roll out. Children should not have cords or ties on their clothing as these could wrap around their necks and choke them. Sheets and blankets must not cover a baby's head. Place a baby at the bottom of a cot and then tuck the blankets in, so that the baby does not slip under the covers. |
| Hot drinks | Children can be badly burned if they pull a hot drink onto themselves | Adults should never drink hot drinks near children. When putting drinks down, they should be placed at the back of the work surface, out of the reach of children. |
| Toys and equipment | Children can trip and fall over toys which are lying around on the floor. Children can pull toys and equipment onto themselves if they are stacked up high | Tidy away toys and equipment that are not being used. Place toys and equipment tidily in cupboards or in **storage boxes**. Make a space for children to play safely. |
| Stairs | Children can fall down stairs or trip over toys left lying on the stairs | Never leave anything on stairs. If children are young, fit **safety gates** to the top and bottom of the stairs, to stop children climbing up and down the stairs without an adult. |
| High chairs | Children can fall from high chairs and be injured | Always use a **safety harness** and supervise children. |
| Pans on cookers | Children can pull the pans onto themselves or touch the heat and be burned | Use a **cooker guard**, which will stop children from touching the heat or the pans. |

**Table 11.1** Safety equipment required to avoid hazards in the home

**Assessment task 3**

In your booklet, write a list of five hazards in the home. For each one, say what you will need to do to keep the child safe.

Illness or death can be caused by children touching or playing with dangerous products, or swallowing harmful chemicals such as medicines or cleaning products.

## Medicine and tablet safety

Medicines are often brightly coloured and children might think that they are sweets, but they can be very dangerous if eaten. It is VERY important to keep all medicine and tablets out of the reach of children.

Too much medicine or the wrong medicine can hurt or even kill. Medicines that are meant for adults can make children very ill.

Here are some very important safety points to remember:

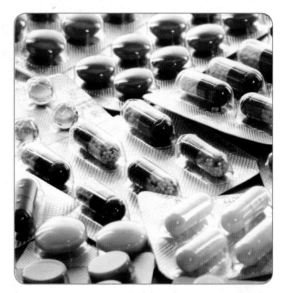

**Figure 11.4** Medicines must be kept away from children

- Medicines should be stored in a locked cupboard or box and kept out of the reach of children.

- Medicine bottles should have child-safety screw tops.

- The correct amount of medicine should be given at right times.

- Always keep medicines in the packet or container they came in.

- Read and keep any labels or instruction leaflets that come with the medicine – this will give you information about what to do if there is a problem.

- Never give prescribed medicines to other people even if they seem to have a similar illness.

- Old medicine and tablets should be taken back to the chemist, so that they can be destroyed.

- Do not put medicines in the sink or toilet. They can poison the water and make people and animals sick.

## Safety equipment outside the setting 2.3

Children can be badly injured if they are not looked after properly when taken outdoors. The spidergrams in Figure 11.5 show some ways to keep children safe when outdoors.

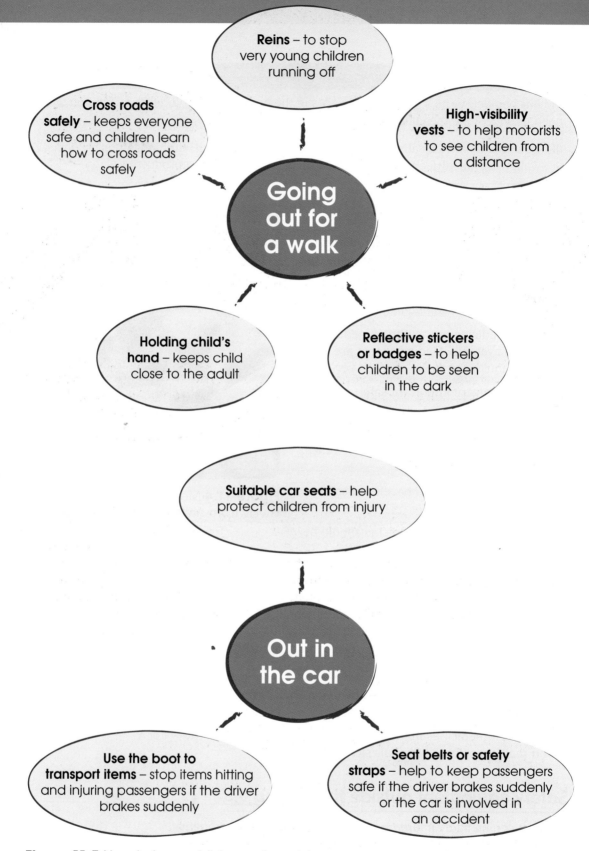

**Figure 11.5** How to keep children safe outdoors

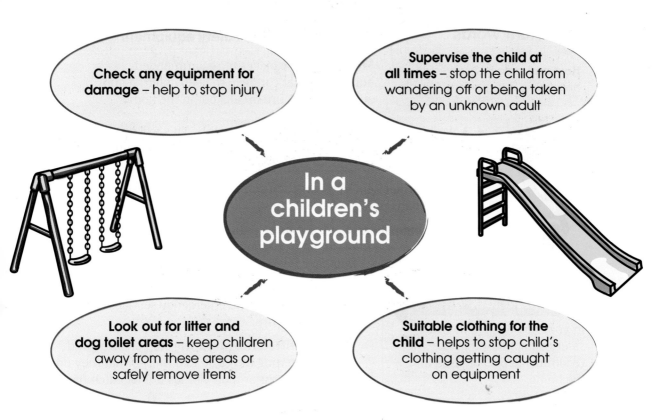

**Figure 11.5** Continued

**Assessment task 4**

Look at car safety for children. Cut out pictures of car seats suitable for a baby aged one month and a child aged five years, and stick them into your booklet. Write down why it is important to get the right type of seat for a child.

**Assessment task 5**

In your booklet, write about how you can keep a child safe on a walk to the local shop. Include some of the hazards and the ways to keep children safe.

## Fire safety in the home ③

Every year in the UK there are tens of thousands of accidental house fires. These cause around 20 people to be burned or injured every day, and some people die as a result of their injuries. Breathing in smoke is the greatest cause of injury or death.

Children are often very interested in fire, so it is important both to keep them safe and try and teach them about the dangers of fire.

It is very important to think about fire safety, and whenever possible remove the risk of children and adults being injured through fire.

## Important words

**Recommended** – suggested because it is important.

## Recommended fire safety equipment 3.1

There are a few pieces of recommended equipment that can help to keep children and adults safe if a fire breaks out in the home:

- **A working smoke alarm** that is tested weekly. This will sound loudly if smoke is in the air, and allows people in the house to get out quickly and safely.

- **A fire blanket** kept in the kitchen can be used to put over the top of burning pans to put out the flames.

- **Fire extinguishers**: there are three main types of fire extinguisher: powder, water and foam. Fire extinguishers are only recommended to be used by people who have been trained to use them safely.

- **A working telephone** should be available to call 999 to contact the emergency services in the event of a fire.

- **A well-fitted fireguard** will stop children and adults getting too close to a fire, so that they do not get burnt or their clothes do not catch fire.

### Assessment task 6

In your booklet, list the fire safety equipment that is recommended to be used in the home.

## Fire hazards in the home 3.2

There are many ways that fires can be started accidentally within the home.

- **Cigarettes**: more people die in fires caused by lit cigarettes, matches and lighters than in fires caused by anything else. Children should be kept away from cigarettes and matches.

- **Candles** and lit decorations cause a growing number of house fires, and should not be used around children.

- **Overloaded sockets**: too many electrical appliances plugged into one socket can overload it, which can lead to electrical equipment catching fire. Children should never touch an electric socket or cable.

- **Cooking**: more than half of fires in the home start because of something to do with cooking. Children should **never** be left alone in a kitchen when cooking is being done.

- **Gas and coal fires**: although it is unusual for these heating appliances to cause house fires, children are at a high risk of being burned if they are too near to them. A fireguard should always be used when the fire is lit.

### Assessment task 7

In your booklet, write down three fire hazards in the home.

**Figure 11.6** Fire safety equipment for the home

## What to do in the event of a fire ③.③

It is important that adults think about what to do if a fire breaks out in the house, especially if it is during the night.

**Make your home safe for children**

The government has given specific advice about keeping children safe from fire:

- Do not leave children on their own in a room where there is a fire risk.
- Keep matches, lighters and candles in a place where children cannot see or reach them. Put child locks on cupboards.
- Put a child-proof fireguard in front of an open fire or heater.
- Do not let children play or leave toys near a fire or heater.
- Keep portable heaters in a safe place where they cannot be knocked over.
- Never leave children alone in the kitchen when you are cooking, and never let them play near the cooker.
- Make sure electrical appliances are switched off when they are not being used.

## A plan

It is important to have a plan so that if a fire breaks out you do not panic. The plan should include:

- working out how you would safely get everyone out of your home if there was a fire, and making sure everyone in the building knows the plan (including visitors and babysitters)

- letting children hear the smoke/fire alarm so that they know what it sounds like and what they should do if they hear the alarm

- practising getting out of the building quickly with any children

- keeping all doors and passages clear at all times of the day and night

- checking for fire hazards in your home before you go to bed; it takes longer to become aware of a fire when you are asleep.

## Action

If a fire breaks out, follow these guidelines:

1 If the smoke or fire alarm sounds, you should quickly and safely get everyone out of the building.

2 If anyone is trapped upstairs, they should close the door and put clothes or blankets under the door so that dangerous smoke stays out of the room. They should move close to the window so that they can be seen by the emergency services.

3 Call the emergency services by dialling 999 straight away. Try to stay calm and give your address and details of what is happening.

4 Do not go back into the building until you are told it is safe to do so.

> **Assessment task 8**
>
> In your booklet, write a plan to get children out of the building safely if there is a fire.

## Summary

In this unit you will have learnt that:

- safety symbols help us to choose safe and suitable toys and equipment for children
- cleaning product labels show important information about their safe use
- adults have a big role in keeping children safe, both indoors and outdoors
- there is a range of equipment to keep children safe, both indoors and outdoors
- fire in the home causes injury and death to children and adults every year
- adults should plan and practise how to get children and adults out of the building safely if there was a fire.

# Chapter 12

# CFC 25 Finding out about Forest schools

## What you will learn in this unit

You will gain a greater understanding of:

- what a Forest school is
- how being outdoors helps children to be healthy
- the places that children can safely learn outdoors
- ways in which children can learn in the outdoor environment
- what kind of skills children can develop when they are learning outside.

## What is a Forest school? 1.1

The main features of a Forest school are as follows:

- The children spend most of the day learning in a woodland outdoors, instead of inside in a classroom.

- Children spend time exploring and looking at nature while they are in the forest. They can touch the leaves and trees instead of just looking at them in pictures.

- Children also have the opportunity to climb trees, and make dens to play in and keep dry in the rain.

- Children are outdoors even in the rain and snow; they just have to wear the right clothes to keep themselves warm and dry.

- Children can see the changes through the seasons; for example, in springtime most trees begin to blossom and the forest becomes green.

- Children learn lots of new social skills, including learning to communicate with other children when they are doing an activity together; for example, deciding what materials to use when they are building a den in the woods.

- Children learn teamwork skills; for example, deciding which route to take when they are walking through the woods. The children will all have to agree to go the same way so that everyone is together and no child is left to wander off alone.

- Children have the chance to explore outdoors in the fresh air. They will be able to experience the weather; for example, feeling the rain bouncing on their waterproof jackets or seeing the wind blowing the leaves around.

- There is usually some sort of shelter where children can relax.

- Children are able to use a range of tools such as spades, saws or ropes.

**Figure 12.1** The natural world is a rich environment for children's learning

### Assessment task 1

Design a poster which shows the main features that can be found in a Forest school.

## Choosing an outdoor learning environment 2.1 2.2

There are many outdoor areas that children will enjoy exploring and where they can learn about the environment. Children can learn lots of different skills and gain knowledge about the world they live in from being in different types of outdoor area.

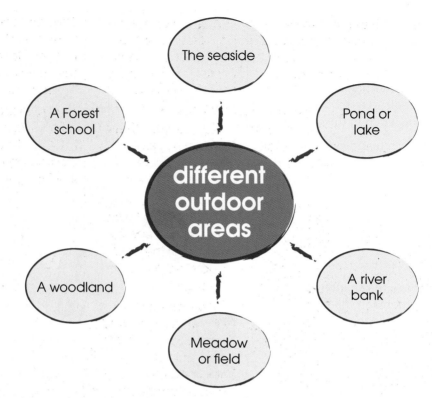

**Figure 12.2** Different types of outdoor area

| The area where learning takes place | What do these areas look like? | What can children learn in the outdoor area? | What new skills can children develop in the outdoor area? |
|---|---|---|---|
| Woodland areas | This is an area mostly covered with trees, shrubs and flowers. | Children can learn about the seasons and how the woodland changes. They can learn about insects, birds and woodland animals, such as woodlice, beetles, badgers, foxes and owls. | Children can learn how to walk carefully without damaging the woodland. Children can learn to safely climb and move through the wooded area. They can learn how to make dens, build shelters and use tools safely. |

**Table 12.1** How the outdoor environment can boost children's learning

| Fields and meadows | Fields are large areas of grassland and can sometimes be used to grow crops.<br><br>Meadows are usually left to grow naturally and can be full of wild flowers. | Children can learn by looking at the crops and flowers, and observe how they grow and change.<br><br>They can use their senses by gently touching and smelling the wild flowers.<br><br>Children can learn about the seasons and how the fields and meadows change.<br><br>They can learn about growing and about insects, birds and animals, such as field mice, swallows and hedgehogs. | Children can learn how to walk carefully without damaging the fields and meadows.<br><br>They can learn to watch bugs and insects without damaging the area in which they live. |
| --- | --- | --- | --- |
| Ponds and streams | A pond is a small area of water which can be created naturally or man-made. | A pond is a good place to find many living animals, and children can find insects or plants in or around the pond. Children can observe the birds and other animals that visit the pond for rest and food.<br><br>They can look for fish if the pond is large enough.<br><br>They can learn the life cycle of butterflies and frogs. | Children can learn to use fishing nets to look at pond life. They can balance on rocks if it is safe to do so. Children can use magnifying glasses to look at tiny pond life. They can learn how to be responsible for their own safety by following rules about safe play. An example of this is when children are free to play by the water edge as long as they are wearing a float jacket.<br><br>Children learn how to use tools safely. |

| Forests | A large area covered with trees. Some forests have trees that are very tall, which means that they block the sun out, and very little sunlight gets to the ground. | Children can learn about how trees change through the seasons, and which leaves and fruits belong to different trees. Children learn by walking through the forest, watching what is happening around them. Children can use all of their senses to learn about the forest area. They will smell the woodland, listen to the animals and birds and feel the textures of the forest. | Children can learn how to use magnifying glasses to closely watch how bugs and insects move. Children can learn how to make shelters and dens. Tree climbing and log balancing can be practised by children. Learning how to navigate through a thick forest without getting lost is a good skill to learn. Children can track signs of forest animals such as foxes or badgers, and use tools safely. |
|---|---|---|---|

**Table 12.1** Continued

## Safety issues in an outdoor environment  2.3

Safety is very important and must be thought about at all times. All activities and forest areas are checked for dangers by staff: this is called **risk assessing**.

- Children must never be left alone, and should always be supervised closely by adults.

- When using tools such as spades and saws, children are shown how to use them carefully and safely.

- When safely making fires, children are watched closely by the adults.

- **At all times** children are encouraged to think about what they are doing and how to do it safely to ensure that they do not get hurt.

Safety issues and things the adults need to remember:

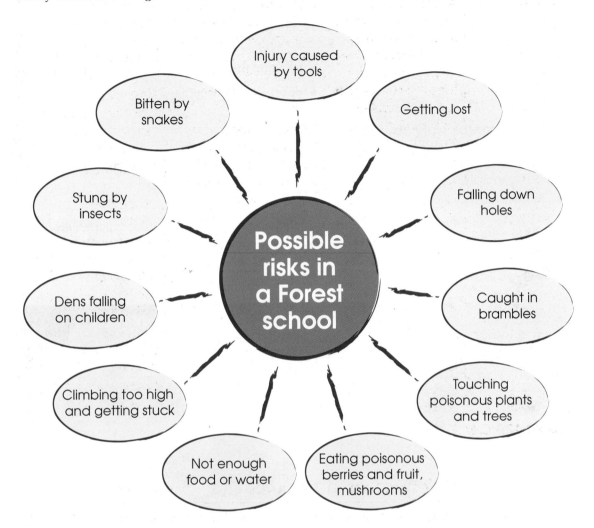

**Figure 12.3** Possible risks in a Forest school

**Assessment task 2** ✓

Using Table 12.1 and Figure 12.2, make an information leaflet about outdoor learning environments.

1. List the different types of outdoor environments where children can learn.

2. Describe in more detail one outdoor area where children could learn.

3. List the possible dangers, and write down how to keep children safe in this area.

## Outdoor projects

There are many projects that can be enjoyed by children in outdoor areas. These could include the following:

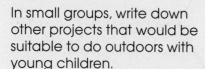

**Task** ✏

In small groups, write down other projects that would be suitable to do outdoors with young children.

- learning the life cycles of butterflies or frogs
- observing the woodland through the seasons
- building a den
- building a dam in a stream
- planting and growing
- weather watching.

Projects can be both enjoyable and full of new learning experiences for children. Projects can last for just a few hours or up to a few months; for example, a short project could be building a den, but a much longer project could be recording weather patterns over a few months.

**Figure 12.4** Building a den provides many opportunities for learning

---

**Assessment task 3** ✔

Using either one of the projects you have written down or one taken from the list above:

1. Write a description of the project, saying what the children will do.

2. Write a list of what children might learn during this project.

3. Write down two skills which children might learn during the project.

---

## Benefits to children of learning outdoors 4.1

From completing this unit you will have learnt that there are many benefits to children of learning in different outdoor areas. Children are learning by using all of their senses, and are developing new skills. These could be physical skills such as tree climbing, social skills such as teamwork to build a den, learning new words to develop their language skills, or learning about the world around them to support their intellectual development.

In the outdoor areas, children usually feel they have more freedom and space to run around and explore. This can give children a sense of emotional wellbeing.

### Important words

**Emotional wellbeing** – having happiness in yourself and feeling positive.

### Assessment task 4

Design a poster using pictures or drawings to show all the benefits for children from learning outdoors. (You could use the table and project to get your information, as well as looking on the internet or in magazines.)

### Summary

Now that you have come to the end of this unit, you will have learnt that:

- there are many different types of outdoor areas where children can explore and learn
- Forest schools can be very interesting places for children to learn new skills
- adults should think carefully about children's safety when they are in outdoor areas
- the outdoor area is a good place for adults to support children's learning
- there are many benefits to children of learning in outdoor areas
- young children can learn lots of new things from outdoor activities when adults support their learning.

# Chapter 13

# CFC 26 Craft activities for young children

## What you will learn in this unit

You will gain an understanding of:

- craft activities which can be suitable for children (aged from six months to five years)
- the benefits of craft activities for young children
- the health and safety risks that must be considered when providing craft activities for young children
- the adult's role in keeping children safe during craft activities.

## Craft activities for young children 1.1 1.2

Craft activities are enjoyed by most young children. They can be an interesting and fun way to spend time with other children and adults. Very young children often like to use paints and crayons at home, and use glue and paper to make pictures at playgroups. In the early years setting, children might be given different-sized boxes, paints and shiny materials so that they can make a model of a robot or car.

When choosing a craft activity to do with a young child, it is very important to make sure that it is suitable for the child's age and ability; you have to consider what they can manage to do. For example, a baby of eight months cannot yet use a pair of scissors, so should be given another type of craft activity to do.

### Important words

**Craft activity** – making something with your hands.

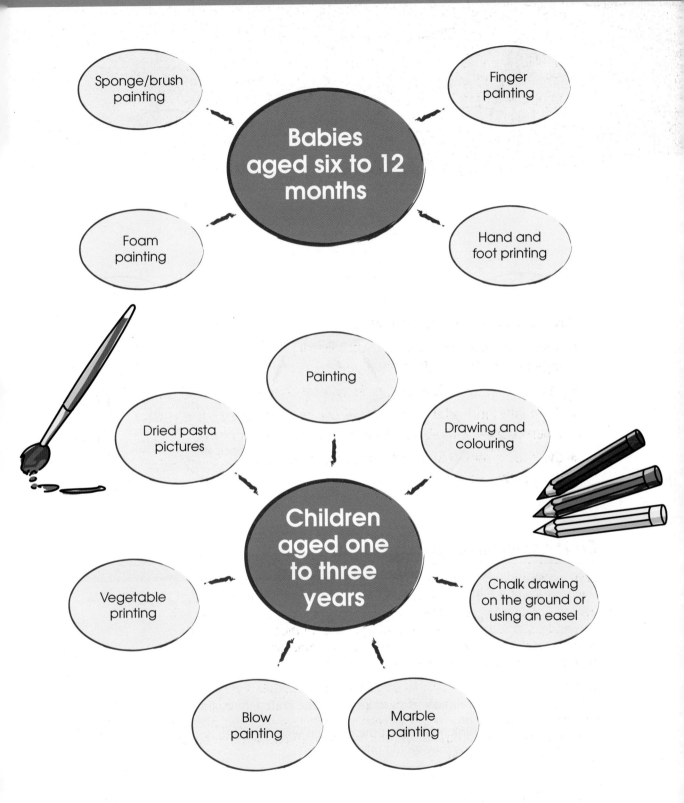

**Figure 13.1** Suitable craft activities for different ages

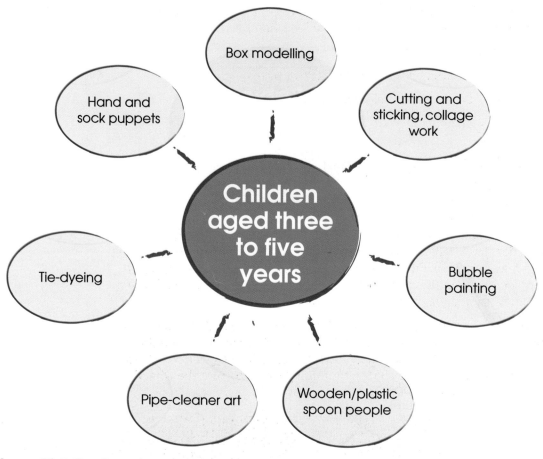

**Figure 13.1** Continued

**Assessment task 1a** ✓

In pairs, think of more craft activities suitable for:

- a baby aged between six and twelve months
- a young child aged between one and two years
- a child aged between three and five years.

Write a short description of one craft activity for each age group.

Think about what the children would need to do the activity, and the steps they would take.

Adults must make sure that they provide babies and young children with the correct equipment to complete the activity. The equipment will depend on the craft activity that has been chosen. For example, a vegetable printing activity will need the following:

- a selection of vegetables and fruit
- different-coloured paints in wide bowls or plates
- large sheets of white or coloured paper
- aprons or an old shirt.

## The benefits of craft activities and what children can learn 1.3 3.1

There are many benefits for children when they take part in craft activities. Craft activities give babies and young children the chance to get messy and have fun. Most craft activities help children to develop good hand and eye coordination, such as when they hold a crayon and move it carefully around the page.

Craft activities can help to build children's confidence and self-esteem, as they can feel proud of the pictures they make. This can be a good time to talk to children and develop their social skills; activities can also help to support their language development, finding words to describe what they are doing (for example, 'the dough feels squishy').

**Figure 13.2** Craft activities can boost children's confidence

Craft activities also provide great opportunities for children to learn new things, such as how long paint takes to dry on the paper, or how much glue you need to use. Children may use different-coloured crayons or different-shaped paper, and the adult can use this chance to support the learning of colours, shapes and even counting.

## Assessment task 1b

In pairs, make a list of all the new things that could be learned through doing the craft activities chosen in the last task. Copy Table 13.1 and fill in the gaps.

| Age of child | Craft activity | Learning opportunities |
|---|---|---|
| | | |
| | | |
| | | |
| | | |
| | | |

**Table 13.1** Learning opportunities provided by craft activities

## Health and safety during craft activities 2.1 2.2

There are some health and safety risks with craft activities for young children, which need to be thought about by adults before the activity. These could be things that could cause an accident or injure a child. Take, for example, a pair of scissors:

- Scissors can be dangerous, even ones especially made for young children.

- They are often made from a hard material and are long, thin and slightly pointed.

- They may cause an injury if a young child puts them inside their own mouth, or if one child uses the scissors to poke another.

This is not something that would definitely happen during an activity, but it is something that should be thought about and considered by the adult.

### Important words

**Health and safety risks** – any harm or injury that may take place.

**Figure 13.3** Possible safety risks in craft activities

## Supporting a child to carry out craft activities safely ⓘ

During any activity with young children, the adult should be aware of accidents that may happen. Even with careful planning and thought, certain things can go wrong. Children often put things in their mouths, or use equipment in the wrong way, such as waving a paintbrush like a sword. It is important that children are watched carefully when they are doing any sort of craft activity, so that if the child begins to use equipment in the wrong way or spills something, you can safely deal with the situation.

Always make sure that the tools and equipment are in good condition and suitable for the craft activity.

Adults working with babies and young children need to think about health and safety risks before doing an activity with them. When a risk has been identified by the adult, they can then think of ways to deal with the risk and stop an accident from happening.

## Assessment task 2

Complete Table 13.2, which lists health and safety risks when providing craft activities, how to deal with these risks, and in which ways the adult can support babies and young children.

| Health and safety risks when providing craft activities for young children | How to deal with the health and safety risks | The support which children might need when doing the craft activity |
|---|---|---|
| Using sharp scissors  | Make sure that safety scissors are being used.<br><br>Make sure that left-handed children have the appropriate scissors. | Discuss safe ways of using the scissors with the children.<br><br>Observe the activity to make sure that they are being used correctly. |
| | | |
| | | |
| | | |

**Table 13.2** Health and safety risks during craft activities

## Summary

In this unit you will have learnt that:

- craft activities are enjoyed by most young children
- there are many different types of craft activities that are suitable for young children, and adults need to make sure that the activity is right for the age of the child
- children can learn lots of things when enjoying craft activities, including counting, colours and shapes
- adults should always watch children carefully to keep them safe during craft activities
- it is important to think about any possible risk of children being harmed during the activity, and if necessary change the activity so that it is safe.

# Chapter 14

# 03 Understanding play for early learning

## What you will learn in this unit

You will gain an understanding of:

- the features of a positive learning environment
- how play can help children's learning and development
- the ways in which play activities should meet children's individual needs and avoid stereotyping and discrimination.

## Positive learning environments 1.1

A positive learning environment can be created both indoors (for example, a playroom at a toddler group or a day nursery) and outdoors (for example, outside in a woodland or garden area).

### Features of a positive learning environment

The features that make a positive learning environment are very different for outdoor and indoor settings.

### Important words

**Positive leaning environment** – a room or place that supports children's learning.

**Features of a setting** – the appearance and description of a room or place.

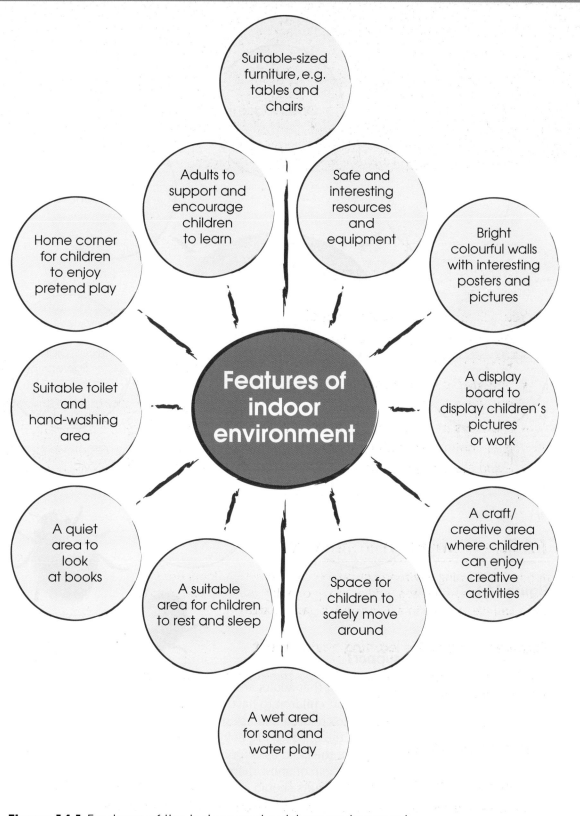

**Figure 14.1** Features of the indoor and outdoor environment

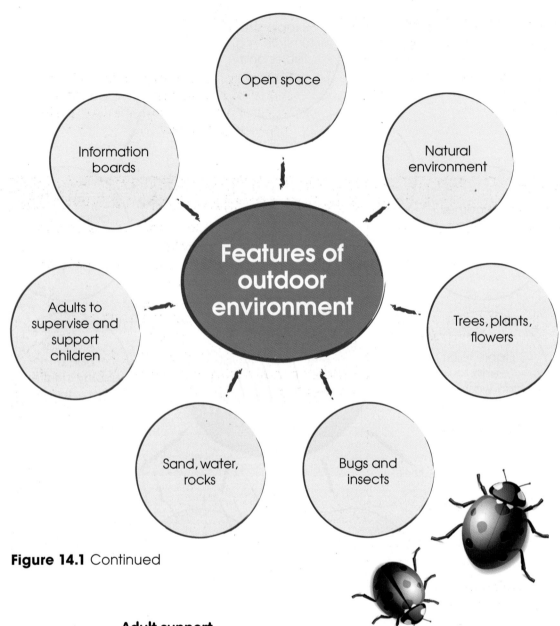

**Figure 14.1** Continued

### Adult support

It is very important that adults are interested in what the children are doing, and support children to have fun, enjoy the activities and stay safe. Adults can talk to children and ask them about the activity, showing interest in what the children are doing. Adults should not take over the child's play, but if the child asks for help or is struggling to do an activity, it is important to help or show them how to do it without completing the activity for them. Adults should support children to stay safe. All children need to take some risks, but the adult needs to make sure the child is as safe as possible whilst taking the risk.

## How a positive environment helps children to learn 1.2

The features of an environment are important for children for many different reasons.

## Task

In small groups, look at Tables 14.1 and 14.2, showing features of indoor and outdoor play environments. Complete the missing information.

| Features of indoor setting | How the features help children's learning |
| --- | --- |
| Suitable-sized furniture | Children are comfortable, so they will be able to concentrate on their activities. Children can safely get on and off the chairs, so they learn to be independent. |
| Interesting posters and pictures on the wall | Children will enjoy looking at the posters and pictures and learning new things. The pictures might be a way of introducing children to new words or starting discussions with the children. |
| A display board | |
| A craft/creative area | |
| A suitable area for children to rest and sleep | |
| A wet area for sand and water play | This area will allow children to play with sand and water safely so that if it goes on the floor children will not slip and fall. |
| Suitable toilet and hand-washing area | To allow children to wash hands after messy play and to be able to use the toilet so that they become independent. |

**Table 14.1** Features of indoor environment

| Features of outdoor setting | How the features help children's learning |
|---|---|
| Different types of weather and changes in temperature | Children learn about what the weather feels like, such as wind and rain. Children understand about wearing suitable clothes to keep warm, cool or dry. |
| Trees to climb, logs to balance on | Risk and challenge. Children learn about keeping themselves safe. |
| Dens to build and use | Learning about construction through play. Learning how to use tools safely. |
| Sand, water and rocks | |
| Information boards | Show pictures and give information about the environment and wildlife. |
| Discovering bugs and insects | |

**Table 14.2** Features of outdoor environment

### Assessment task 1 ✓

In pairs, design a room or outside play area which children aged between three and four years may enjoy using. Draw and label all of the features that contribute to your positive learning environment. When deciding on the important features, think about how each of the features might help and encourage children to learn.

## How play supports early learning 2.1

Play is a very important part of children's learning and development. It is through play that children use their senses to develop new skills and learn about the world around them.

### Important word

**Contribute** – add to.

**Figure 14.2** Playing together supports learning

When children play, they are practising skills they have already learnt and developing new ones. When children play together, they are learning how to share as well as having fun, being occupied by what they are doing, and burning energy while running and playing sports. A great deal of learning takes place that perhaps is not so obvious at first.

Play can support children's development in the following areas:

- physical – many play activities help children to learn new physical skills
- social – many play activities can help children to develop social skills
- emotional – many play activities can help children to understand their emotions
- intellectual – many activities can help children to develop intellectually
- language – many activities help children to learn new words.

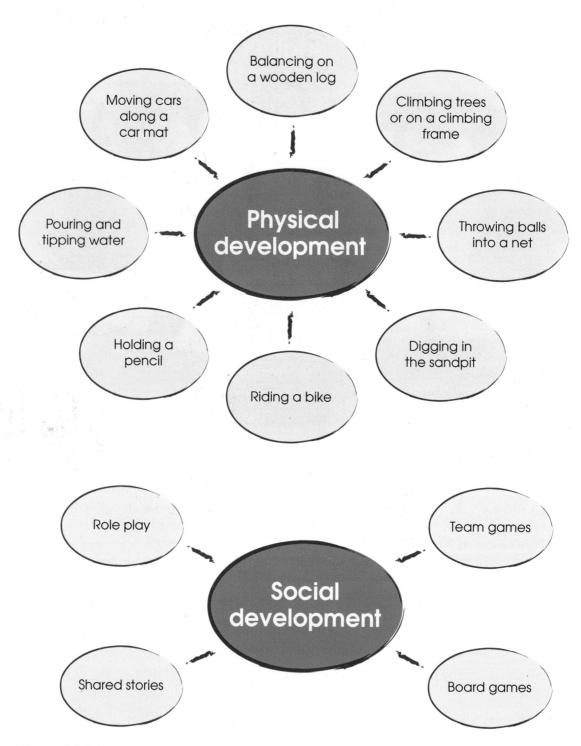

**Figure 14.3** How play supports different areas of development

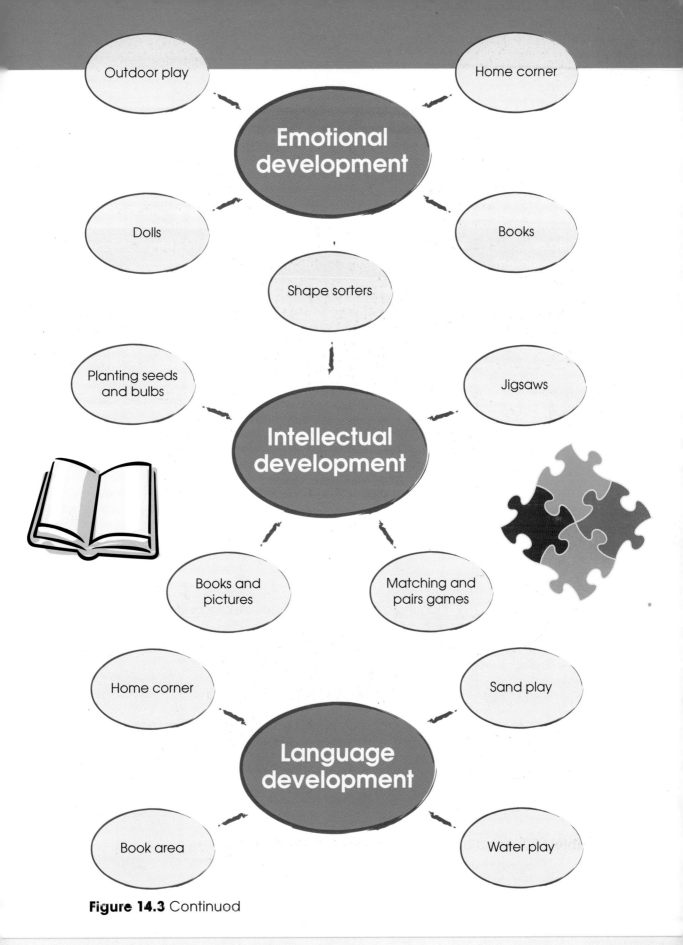

**Figure 14.3** Continuod

Copy out Table 14.3 below. Complete the table by suggesting a second activity for each area of development. Write down how it helps children's learning.

| Area of development | Play activity | How the play activity helps children's learning and development |
|---|---|---|
| Physical development | **1** Balancing on a wooden log<br>**2** | **1** This helps children to develop strong muscles and good balance.<br>**2** |
| Social development | **1** Board games<br>**2** | **1** Agreeing the rules, turn taking, and sharing the dice.<br>**2** |
| Emotional development | **1** Outdoor play<br>**2** | **1** Feeling proud when they have climbed higher in the tree, running around and feeling free.<br>**2** |
| Intellectual development | **1** Planting seeds and caring for them<br>**2** | **1** Understanding what seeds need to grow and observing how they change as they grow.<br>**2** |
| Language development | **1** Sand play<br>**2** | **1** Learning new words such as sprinkle, pat, scoop, tip, rake.<br>Talking to each other as they play.<br>**2** |

**Table 14.3** How play activity supports children's learning

# Avoiding stereotyping and discrimination ③.1

Discrimination is when the environment, materials or activities are not suitable for all children. This may make some children feel left out and not included. It is therefore very important that adults challenge discrimination and make sure that all children feel included. For example, if a child attends the nursery and sees pictures of families from their own cultural background in books and on posters, they will feel included and understand that their culture is valued.

Stereotyping happens when we label people or make judgments about them because of what we see or think. For example, to help children not to stereotype job roles in the home, they should see pictures of a man ironing clothes or a woman mending a car.

## Task

Copy Table 14.4 below about challenging discrimination in play, and fill in the missing gaps.

## Important words

**Challenge discrimination** – when we take action to make sure that no child feels left out or bullied because of what they can do or how they look.

**Stereotyping** – labelling a person without taking the time to understand who they are.

**Discrimination** – to treat one person differently from another person because of their race, colour or whether they are a girl or a boy.

| Description of activity or resource | How we can make sure that this activity or resource challenges stereotyping | How we can make sure that this activity or resource challenges discrimination |
|---|---|---|
| Small world play | The plastic people can be given different jobs; e.g. a girl can be driving a lorry and the boy can be shopping. | The plastic people could have different-coloured skin and be dressed with clothes from different cultures. |
| Jigsaws | | |

| Description of activity or resource | How we can make sure that this activity or resource challenges stereotyping | How we can make sure that this activity or resource challenges discrimination |
|---|---|---|
| Posters | | |
| Home corner | | Have a variety of different types of cooking pots and foods, e.g. woks to cook in and plastic foods from different countries. |
| Dolls | | |
| Books | Having stories and pictures of people with disabilities doing everyday activities such as using the bus, going to work or joining in with sports. | |

**Table 14.4** Ways in which to combat discrimination and stereotyping in children's play

## Summary

Now that you have come to the end of the unit, you will have learnt that:

- many different features of indoor and outdoor environments can support children's learning
- play activities can help children's physical, social, emotional, intellectual and language development
- having a good variety of resources and carefully planned activities will help to challenge stereotyping and discrimination.

# Chapter 15

# HL 1 Healthy living

## What you will learn in this unit

You will gain an understanding of:

- the importance of leading a healthy lifestyle
- how to get involved in doing different activities to keep you healthy
- how well different activities can help to support your healthy lifestyle.

## Understand the importance

## of leading a healthy lifestyle 1.2 2.2

A healthy lifestyle is a way of living that lowers our risk of becoming very ill or dying early. We cannot stop ourselves from getting some diseases, but there are some types of illness such as heart disease or lung cancer that may be avoided by having a healthy lifestyle. Scientists have found out that we can cut our risk of becoming very ill and can live longer by not smoking or drinking too much alcohol, and by taking regular exercise, having a healthy diet, and getting sensible amounts of rest and sleep.

Health is not just about illness and disease. It is also about physical, mental and social wellbeing.

When adults have a healthy lifestyle, they can be seen as positive role models for children. This means that the children will see good lifestyle habits; children copy what they see, so if people working with children have healthy lifestyles, then the children will pick up healthy habits too.

> ### Important words
>
> **Healthy lifestyle** – choosing a healthy way of life.

Sometimes we do not think about whether we have a healthy lifestyle, and we may not exercise enough or eat healthy foods. If we take time to think about the way we live, we can become healthier.

**Figure 15.1** Living healthily makes us feel good about ourselves

## Important words

**Personal log** – a diary that is used to keep a record of your own lifestyle; for example, the food you ate or the exercise you did during a certain day.

## Assessment task 2 ✓

On the next page is an example of a daily diary (personal log). Keep a daily diary like the one below, for three days. Write down the exercise you do, the social activities you take part in, the foods you eat and how much sleep and rest you get.

Caring for Children

| Exercise | Food | Rest and sleep | Social activity |
|---|---|---|---|
| Today I played with my niece in the garden, running and kicking a ball (20 minutes).<br><br>I walked to the bus stop to go to college. I tried to walk quickly so I was 'huffing and puffing' (ten minutes).<br><br>I walked to my gran's house with my niece after college (five minutes each way).<br><br>In the evening I played on the dance mat with my friends (one hour). | Corn flakes, toast, milk and a glass of fresh orange juice (good food).<br><br>Packet of crisps (not good food)<br><br>Vegetable samosa, an apple and water (good food).<br><br>Dried fruit snack.<br><br>Chicken pasta bake with cheese, peas and sweetcorn, yoghurt with berries. Water.<br><br>I drank water throughout the day. | Woke up at 7.30 am (I went to bed at 10.30 pm so I had about nine hours' sleep).<br><br>I sat quietly with my friends during the lunch break. We sat on the grass field and looked at magazines (rested for 35 minutes).<br><br> | I spent the day with my friends at college.<br><br>I played with my niece, who is four years old.<br><br>I went to see my gran. I enjoy talking to her.<br><br>I did my college homework for an hour and then danced on the dance mat with my friends. |

**Table 15.1** A personal log

## The importance of exercise and activity

- Doing physical activity every day, such as swimming, dancing or other sports, is important for the healthy growth, development and wellbeing of children and young people.

- You should try to have at least 60 minutes of physical activity every day, including the kind of activities that make you 'huff and puff'; for example, fast walking or bouncing on a trampoline.

- You should show children that exercise and outdoor activities are enjoyable, so that they will learn that exercise is fun and a good thing to do.

- Lazy or 'still' time is time spent watching television, surfing the internet, chatting to friends on your mobile phone or playing computer games. You should not spend too much time during the day doing these activities, because sitting around and not being active are linked to children and adults becoming overweight or obese.

- If we are too fat, then this is probably because we are eating too much food and not doing enough exercise. Try and be more active and cut out foods that are not healthy, such as fried foods, salty foods and foods which are sugary.

**Important words**

**Improve** – to make better.

**Figure 15.2** Physical activity can be enjoyable

## How can we lead healthy lifestyles?

We can all improve our health and wellbeing if we decide to put in some effort.

Changes to lifestyles could include:

- doing more exercise: activities that keep us fit and healthy can be done alone (such as going for a jog in the morning), or can be done with a friend (such as playing badminton at the local sports centre). We can also get involved in fitness activities as part of a group. These activities could involve playing football in a local team or joining a 'keep fit' or a yoga class at the local gym.

- stopping smoking

- drinking safe amounts of alcohol

- not taking drugs

- eating a healthy, balanced diet as much as possible

- getting enough sleep at night, especially if we need to study or work the next day.

✓

## Assessment task 2

Look at your daily diary (personal log) and think about three things you could change that would make you healthier (for example, you may not do enough exercise, or you may eat lots of sugary foods). When you have chosen three things to try and change, put them into a table such as Table 15.2. The longer you stick to any positive changes you make, the more positive effects you should see.

| Activities to improve my lifestyle | Witness testimony (short description of improvement made and signature) |
|---|---|
| Example: I spend too much time on the internet, so I will try and limit this to one hour each day. I will exercise for 30 minutes more every day for five days this week. | I went to the park to walk my Aunt Jean's dog every evening for half an hour. I did this Monday to Friday (five days). Signed by Jean May 14/09/2011 |
| 1 | |
| 2 | |
| 3 | |

**Table 15.2** Activities for a healthier lifestyle

## Important words

**Witness testimony** – someone else's signature to prove that you have done something.

**Description** – a short report.

**Figure 15.3** A good night's sleep can contribute to a healthy lifestyle

## Rest and sleep

- Sleep is important because it gives your body a chance to rest, and allows it to prepare for the next day.

- Sleep also gives your brain a chance to sort things out. Scientists think that sleep may be the time when the brain sorts and stores information, replaces chemicals, and solves problems.

- The amount of sleep we need depends a lot on our age. Babies sleep a lot – about 14 to 15 hours per day day! But as we get older, most of us need about eight or nine hours of sleep each night.

## Choose water as a drink

- Water is the best way to quench your thirst and hydrate your body (making sure that your body has enough water to work properly).

- Cut down on drinks with added sugar such as soft drinks and other fizzy drinks. These are not so good at hydrating your body, and can cause tooth decay.

- Skimmed or semi-skimmed milk is healthy to drink as it contains lots of nutrients. It is a great source of calcium, which we need to keep our bones strong.

- Eat whole fruit rather than drinking fruit juices, as they can have a lot of sugar in them.

## A healthy diet ③

Figure 15.4 shows the Eatwell plate. It has five food groups:

1 bread, rice, potatoes, pasta and other starchy foods

2 fruit and vegetables

3 milk and dairy foods

4 meat, fish, eggs, beans and other non-dairy sources of protein

5 foods and drinks high in fat and/or sugar.

> **Important words**
>
> **Hydrate** – replace lost water.

Caring for Children

Groups 1, 2, 3 and 4 contain foods that help to keep our bodies healthy. The eatwell plate encourages you to choose foods from the four important food groups every day.

**Figure 15.4** The eatwell plate

Foods and drinks in group 5 are high in fat and/or sugar. They are not good for a healthy diet.

### Eat more fruit and vegetables

- Eating fruit and vegetables every day helps to keep our bodies healthy.

- Try to eat two pieces of fruit and five servings of vegetables every day.

- Have fresh or dried fruit as a snack instead of sugary or salty snacks.

## Personal hygiene

We should all know how to have good personal hygiene.

- When we look clean and smell fresh we feel good, so our self-esteem grows and we can become more confident.

- A bright white smile with clean, healthy teeth can make us look and feel good.

- Healthy hair, skin and nails are signs of good personal hygiene, and are especially important when we are around children.

- Hand washing after using the toilet or before touching food is very important. Lots of harmful germs which we cannot see live on our skin. Some germs can cause sickness, and some sickness is so serious it could make you very unwell and could even kill a baby or small child. Always wash your hands well with warm soapy water before handling any food.

- Having clean clothes and having a shower every day are important. If we do not keep our bodies and clothes clean we could begin to smell. An unpleasant body smell is often caused by having unwashed underarms, so it is important to wash under your arms every day, wear clean clothes and if necessary wear a deodorant to help you to smell fresh.

## Drug awareness

Drugs can change the way our body and mind work.

- Drugs can be very addictive (the feeling that you need to take the drug more and more).

- Some drugs are illegal: it is against the law to take them, and if caught you could get into trouble with the police.

- Taking drugs can also cause mental health problems, which can be very frightening.

- Drugs can harm our bodies and make us ill; for example, some drugs might cause cancer.

- Taking drugs can cost a lot of money. Some people who take drugs get into debt and may even borrow money from loan sharks or break the law and steal.

- Buying drugs might mean that we have to spend time with people who do not care about us, and we may not be safe.

- Taking drugs can upset family life and cause arguments with friends. This can lead to loneliness.

There are lots of places to get help and support for problems with drugs.

Adults must never use drugs when with children. Adults should be positive role models and always do their best to keep children safe.

**Task**

Look on the internet and find out about support for people worried about drugs. A good website to look at is www. talktofrank.com.

## Alcohol awareness

Alcohol is used safely by most people who drink safe amounts of alcohol. However, some people drink too much alcohol. Drinking lots of alcohol at one time is called 'binge drinking'.

- 'Binge drinking' can cause people to be unaware of what they are doing, or even collapse and choke on their own vomit.

- When someone is not in control of their behaviour due to drinking too much, they may have unprotected sex, which can result in unwanted pregnancy or STDs (sexually transmitted diseases).

- Drinking too much alcohol causes serious damage to our bodies, such as liver disease, cancer, high blood pressure or heart attack.

- Drinking can cause changes in behaviour. People sometimes do things that they would usually not do, or go to places that could put them in great danger.

- Some people who are drunk can become very violent towards partners, family or friends.

- Pregnant women who drink can seriously harm their unborn baby, as the alcohol affects the baby growing inside them.

- Parents who drink may not be able to cope with their children or care for them properly.

- People who drink too much can feel very ill afterwards, so they might not go to college or work. This could affect their future career.

There are lots of places to get help and support for problems about drinking too much alcohol.

Adults must never use alcohol when with children. Adults should be positive role models and always do their best to keep children safe.

## Task

Look on the internet and find out about support for people worried about alcohol. A good website to look at is www. nhs.uk/Tools/Pages/Alcoholcalculator.aspx.

## Stop smoking

Smoking can seriously damage our health and the health of people around us. This is why it is important to try to stop smoking.

Stopping smoking will help our health to improve in many ways:

**Figure 15.5** Stopping smoking brings health benefits

- It will cut down the risk of getting heart or lung disease.
- You will protect the health of people around you, especially children who breathe in your 'second-hand' smoke. Children sometimes develop asthma or glue ear from being around cigarette smoke.
- You will help your chances of getting pregnant in the future.
- You will improve your breathing and fitness.
- You will enjoy the taste of food more.
- You will save money.
- The health of your skin and teeth will get better.
- You and your home will smell much fresher.

If you smoke and would like to give up, then your doctor or local health centre will explain about the support that you could get.

Adults should never smoke when working with or around children, and should be positive role models. Cigarette smoke in the air can cause damage to children's young lungs.

### Sexual health

It is important to be aware of our sexual health, and to make sure that we take good care of ourselves. By doing this, we can:

- respect ourselves and the choices which we make
- understand that it is important to say 'no' if we are not ready to have a sexual relationship
- look after our own bodies and our emotional wellbeing
- avoid catching sexually transmitted diseases or other harmful infections that can be passed from one person to another during unprotected sex
- avoid unwanted pregnancy.

The more facts you know about sex and relationships, the more confident you will feel. There is much information available, especially on the internet. Two very good websites are www.nhs.uk/worthtalkingabout and www.nhs.uk/livewell.

Other clinics and health professionals who offer useful information about sex, safer sex, contraception, pregnancy and sexually transmitted infections (STIs) are:

- a GP or nurse
- a midwife or health visitor
- a community contraceptive clinic
- a sexual health clinic
- a chemist or pharmacist.

People aged under 25 can also go to a young person's service, such as a Connexions Centre, or to Brook Advisory Centre.

## Review the activities undertaken to maintain a healthy lifestyle

### Important words

**Review** – look back and see how well something has worked.

### Assessment task 3

Complete the personal log so that you can review each of the activities you have tried to make improvements to your lifestyle.

| Activity | What went well / how improvements were made | How the activity could be improved | Two more activities to support a healthy lifestyle |
|----------|---------------------------------------------|------------------------------------|---------------------------------------------------|
|          |                                             |                                    |                                                   |
|          |                                             |                                    |                                                   |
|          |                                             |                                    |                                                   |
|          |                                             |                                    |                                                   |

**Table 15.3** Reviewing your activities

## Summary

In this unit you will have learnt that:

- a healthy lifestyle is a way of living that keeps us fit and well
- a healthy lifestyle includes exercise, good food and enough sleep and rest
- drinking too much alcohol, taking drugs and smoking can cause serious illness or death
- children need to see adults with healthy lifestyles, as this will help them to learn how to stay fit and healthy.

# Chapter 16

# CFC 20 Healthy eating for families

## What you will learn in this unit

You will gain an understanding of:

- the importance of a balanced diet
- how families can eat well
- special food requirements for some people
- how to handle and store food safely.

## The importance of a balanced diet 1.1 1.2 1.3

### The main food groups

To help our bodies to grow and stay healthy, we need to eat a range of healthy foods. This is called a 'balanced diet', and to have a balanced diet, we should eat foods from the five main food groups every day. These groups are:

- bread, other cereals and potatoes
- milk and dairy products
- meat, fish and alternatives
- fruit and vegetables
- foods containing fat and/or sugar.

### Important words

**Main food groups** – foods which are similar can be grouped together.

**Important words**

**Nutrients** – these are contained within foods and do a very important job in the body to keep people healthy.

**Antioxidant** – these work to reverse the effects of pollution on the body.

Foods in each of the groups have different benefits for the body:

- **Carbohydrates** give us energy.
- **Proteins** help with growth and repair.
- **Fats** help the body to use the vitamins and minerals found in foods.
- **Vitamins and minerals** help every part of the body to grow and develop healthily, such as healthy bones, strong teeth, clear skin, healthy heart, etc.

The eatwell plate on page 131 shows the food groups which appear in a balanced diet.

### What is a balanced diet?

Table 16.1 shows all of the main nutrients that make up a balanced diet. It shows the food which the nutrients can be found in, and the benefits for the body.

| Nutrient | Foods it is found in | Benefits for the body |
|---|---|---|
| Carbohydrate | Bread, pasta, couscous, flour, potatoes and bananas | Gives the body energy |
| Protein | Meat, eggs, fish, milk and other dairy products. For vegetarians/vegans, wheat, oats, pulses, lentils, tofu and soya products (e.g. Quorn burgers) | Helps the body to repair cells. Helps the body to grow and develop well |
| Fats | Butter, margarine, vegetable oil, fish and dairy products | Gives the body energy. Helps the body to be able to use vitamins A and D |
| Vitamin A | Carrots, milk, apricots, oily fish and margarine | Good for healthy eyes and clear eyesight |
| Vitamin B | Bread, meat, yeast, pasta, flour, rice and noodles | Good for a healthy nervous system. Helps the body to release energy from other foods |

**Table 16.1** The main nutrients of a balanced diet

| Nutrient | Foods it is found in | Benefits for the body |
|---|---|---|
| Vitamin C | Oranges, lemons, yams, grapefruits, blackcurrants, kiwis and potatoes | Good for healthy gums and skin |
| Vitamin E | Vegetable oil, green leafy vegetables (e.g. spinach), nuts and wheatgerm | Works as an **antioxidant**, protecting the eyes, liver and skin tissues from environmental pollution |
| Vitamin K | Most fresh vegetables, yoghurt, lean meat and eggs | Helps the blood to clot: after an injury it helps the bleeding to slow down and eventually stop. Keeps bones strong and healthy |
| Iron  | Red meat, broccoli, spinach, pak choi, egg yolk, plain chocolate and dried fruits | Helps the blood to carry oxygen through the body. During pregnancy the mother's iron helps the baby's brain to develop and work properly |
| Calcium | Milk, cheese, butter, yoghurt and other dairy products, cereals and grains | Good for healthy bones and teeth. Also helps to keep our hearts healthy |

**Table 16.1** Continued

## Task

Write down everything you ate yesterday. Do you think that you ate a balanced diet? Look at the food group plate; did you eat the right amounts of nutrients to give you a balanced diet?

## The effect of diet on health

At different times in our lives, our bodies have different nutritional needs. The foods which we eat sometimes need to change to give us the correct balanced diet.

**Example!**

Most children and teenagers grow quickly, so they need to have more protein and carbohydrate. Breastfeeding mothers should have slightly more fats in their diet as this helps them to produce the milk for the baby.

**Assessment task  1**

Using paper plates:

1. On the back of a paper plate, write down the meaning of a balanced diet.

2. Divide the plate into the five main food groups, and list a few foods that would go into each group.

3. List five ways in which eating a balanced diet can keep a person healthy.

## Good eating habits for families 2.1

### The importance of family mealtimes

Families can lead very busy lives and sometimes do not spend much time together. This can make some members of a family feel that they are not talking to each other enough. Mealtimes can be a good time for families to sit and eat together, as it will give them the chance to talk to each other.

**Figure 16.1** Family mealtimes are important

## Task

Think about mealtimes in your house:

- Do you eat meals with your family?
- Do you have good eating habits?
- Write down what you can do to set a good example for a child at a dinner table.

Mealtimes spent together as a family also help family members to:

- share thoughts and feeling or worries they may have (for example, how you are doing at college)
- talk about the food they eat (for example, talking about healthy food will teach children about how to stay healthy)
- teach younger children table manners (for example, sitting up at the table and using utensils such as knives, forks or chopsticks)
- tempt children to try foods they have not eaten before (for example, a child who eats lots of sweet foods might be tempted to try vegetables if they see an older brother or sister eating them).

### Assessment task 2

1. Draw a spider diagram showing four reasons why it is important for families to eat together regularly.

2. Draw another spider diagram showing ways that adults can encourage children to eat healthy foods.

3. Draw or write down one example of a healthy meal that could be given to a child (think about including foods from the five food groups).

Regular meals which families eat together can be an important and comforting part of a child's daily routine. It is not only dinner that can be eaten together, but breakfast too. Breakfast is a very important meal that gives us the energy that we need to start the day. Cars need fuel to get from one place to another; our bodies are the same, and our fuel is food.

# How to encourage children to eat healthily 2.2

There are many ways to encourage children to eat well and choose healthy foods:

- Make healthy choices interesting. Many recipe books show simple, healthy meals and snacks which look inviting and attractive for children to eat.

- You can cut food into interesting shapes, or make a face using the ingredients. Also try giving food special names, such as 'cool carrots' and 'brilliant broccoli'.

**Figure 16.2** Healthy snacks can be fun!

- Allow children to get involved. Helping with the shopping can teach children about how to recognise healthy products. Older children can look at the food labels, and even see which nutrients the food contains.

- Home-cooked meals usually provide healthy options. Children can watch food being prepared and cooked using healthy ingredients. 'Fast food' usually contains more fat, sugar and salt than home cooking.

- Children like to copy people around them, so adults should always try to be positive role models. Eat healthily in front of children so that they can see how important it is. Also, talk about healthy food using positive language.

- Make healthy snacks for those hungry moments – bowls of fresh and dried fruits, or chopped, raw vegetables with vegetable dips and olives.

- Try not to give children too many snacks between meals or let them fill up on fizzy drinks. This will spoil their appetite for healthy meals.

Avoid using food as a reward for good behaviour or as a bribe to get a child to do something. This may cause them to develop unhealthy eating habits.

## Healthy meals for children

It is important to spend time thinking about how to make healthy meals for children. Adults can then be sure that the children are getting a good, balanced diet. Children's diets should also have enough energy (calories) to help them grow and develop healthily.

Some things that need to be included in healthy meals include:

- up to five servings of fruit and vegetables every day
- foods that have iron in them, such as meat and fish, or rice and lentils for children who do not eat meat
- foods that have calcium in them, such as dairy products
- starchy food – potatoes, pasta and brown bread are a better way of getting energy than sugary foods
- whole cow's milk for children from 12 months old. Diluted fresh fruit juice with a meal is a good way of getting vitamin C. Children should drink plenty of water if they are thirsty.

## Task

Which of these meals do you think has the most nutrients in it, and why?

- sausage and mashed potatoes, water to drink
- tuna sandwiches, green peppers, cheese and milk
- spaghetti with cheese and butter, and a fizzy drink
- egg and chips, water to drink
- fish fingers, spaghetti and a fizzy drink.

## Special food requirements for different groups ③.①

In most countries there are people who cannot eat certain foods because of health or religious reasons. Adults working with young children need to understand the different diets, religious beliefs, cultures and lifestyles of families, so that they can support their wishes, special diets, customs and eating habits.

### Food restrictions for religious groups

People from different cultures or religious groups may have particular foods that they prefer to eat. The food that they eat will often be different because of their individual needs and beliefs.

> **Important words**
>
> **Food restrictions** – when a certain type of food should not be handled or eaten for health or religious reasons.

## Example!

Examples of these religious groups are:

1 Hindus (Hinduism)
2 Muslims (Islam)
3 Buddhists (Buddhism)
4 Rastafarians (Rastafarianism)
5 Jews (Judaism)
6 Christians (Christianity).

### Hindus

People who practise the Hindu religion do not usually eat beef (meat from a cow). This is because Hindus believe that the cow is a sacred or holy animal that should never be eaten. Strict Hindus will not eat meat or even eggs, as they are also seen as having life. Fat such as lard is not eaten, as it is an animal fat.

**Figure 16.3** Hindus do not eat beef, and many do not eat meat at all

Caring for Children

### Rastafarianism

People who follow the Rastafarian religion believe that it is very important to live a pure life and eat simple foods. This means that they may prefer to live close to nature and grow fresh food on the land. Rastafarians like to keep their bodies pure and healthy, so may choose not to drink alcohol, tea and coffee. There are also rules about the fish and meat they can eat, so many rastafarians choose to follow a vegan diet.

### Buddhists

Most Buddhists choose to become vegetarians so that they can avoid harming or killing any animals. Some Buddhists do not eat fish for the same reason.

### Jews

Many people who practise the Jewish religion follow certain rules about food. One rule is to only prepare and eat food that is **kosher** (prepared according to Jewish law). Like Muslims, Jews do not eat pork.

### Muslims

People who follow the Muslim religion will usually only prepare and eat food which is **halal**. This means that the animal has been slaughtered in a way which is approved by Islam. Muslims do not eat pork, as it is not seen as a 'clean' animal.

**Figure 16.4** Celebrating different religious festivals can be fun for young children and support their knowledge of different cultures

There are no particular dietary requirements for Christian people, but certain foods are important for religious festivals such as Easter and Shrove Tuesday, also known as Pancake Day.

**Assessment task 3a** ✓

Make a poster that gives information on the foods that should not be eaten by people from four religious groups.

## Special dietary requirements 3.2

As well as understanding about foods which people do or do not eat for religious reasons, we also need to be aware of the special diets that some people follow because of health reasons and lifestyle choices.

Some individuals or families may choose not to eat any meat or fish. They may choose to follow a vegetarian or a vegan diet.

> **Important words**
>
> **Special diet** – when a person has a food restriction, so can only eat the foods which they are allowed.

### Vegetarian diet

Vegetarians do not eat meat. They usually prefer to eat food that comes from plants, such as fruit and vegetables. Vegetarians often eat grains, nuts and seeds with the vegetables. These may include rice, lentils or pasta. Vegetarians may eat dairy produce such as cheese and yoghurt and also eggs.

### Vegan diet

People following a vegan diet do not eat meat, fish, eggs or any dairy produce. Many vegans choose not to eat anything that has been made using any part of the animal. This may include animal fats, wine, sauces and even honey because it is made by the bee.

Many vegans do not wear leather or fur, as both of these products are made from animal skin.

## Food allergies 3.3

Having a food allergy means that eating or sometimes touching a certain food causes a person to be ill. If a person has an allergy to a certain food, they should avoid eating it. An **allergic reaction** can happen when somebody eats the food they are allergic to, and becomes ill. The reaction could be, for example, a headache, runny nose or itchy eyes.

The most common foods that children are allergic to are:

- milk
- peanuts and nuts from trees
- eggs
- wheat
- fish (including shellfish: mussels, prawns and crab).

### Important words

**Allergy** – when a person becomes ill after eating or touching a certain food.

**Allergic reaction** – when somebody eats food that they are allergic to.

### Assessment task 3b ✓

1. Write down what vegetarians do and do not eat in their diet.

2. Cut out pictures of three foods that can cause some people to have allergic reactions.

## How to handle and store food safely 4.1

### Personal hygiene, handling and storing food safely

It is very important to have very good personal hygiene when you are preparing or handling food.

### Important words

**Food handling** – buying, storing and preparing food correctly, so that it is safe to eat.

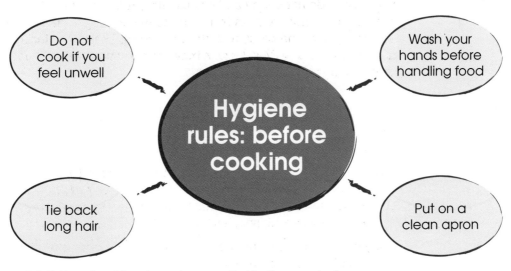

**Figure 16.5** Excellent hygiene is essential in the workplace

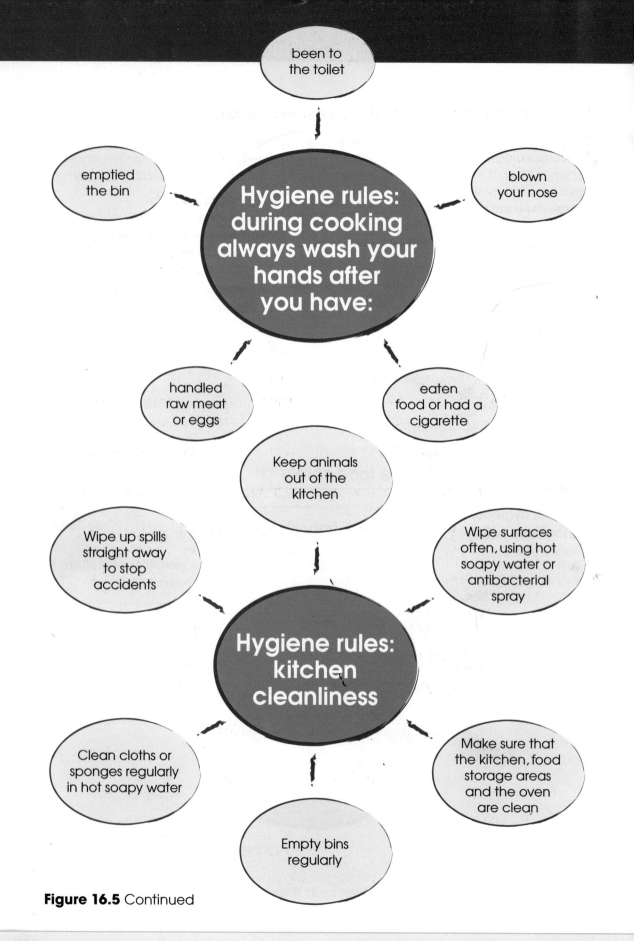

**Figure 16.5** Continued

## Food storage and preparation to stop cross-contamination 4.2 4.3

It is very important to store food safely, so that the food is good to eat and free from germs and bacteria. One hazard of poor food storage is cross-contamination. Some foods are not safe to eat raw because they have germs on them which are removed only during cooking, which then makes the food safe to eat. Cross-contamination happens when the germs from raw foods are passed on to cooked foods, which are then eaten. This can make you very ill.

> ### Important words
>
> **Cross-contamination** – germs or bacteria from one type of food spread to another food.

### Hygiene rules: to avoid cross-contamination

- Defrost frozen food before cooking if required.
- Make sure that food is cooked all the way through, especially meat and fish.
- Keep hot food hot and cold food cold.
- Keep separate knives, dishes and chopping boards for raw and cooked foods to stop cross-contamination.
- Wrap or cover food, and put it away in the fridge or cupboard as soon as it is cool.
- Make sure that raw meat and fish are kept at the bottom of the fridge to stop them dripping onto cooked food and causing cross-contamination.

### Assessment task 4 ✔

You have been asked to help prepare food for a child's party. You will be making: egg sandwiches, falafels, hummus, sushi, cheese chunks, tomatoes, cucumber slices, jelly and ice cream. There will be fruit juice to drink.

1. Write down three reasons why you should wash your hands before starting to prepare this food.

2. Write down one food storage rule you should follow to keep food safe to eat.

3. Write down one way in which this food can be prepared safely.

4. Write down three ways in which you can stop cross-contamination of raw and cooked foods.

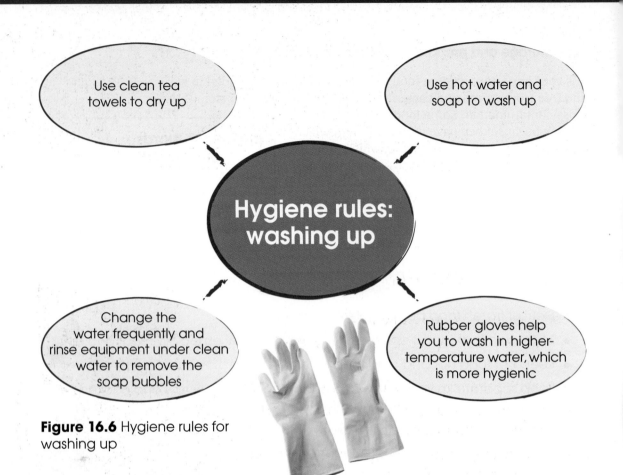

**Figure 16.6** Hygiene rules for washing up

The diagram shows "Hygiene rules: washing up" with the following rules:
- Use clean tea towels to dry up
- Use hot water and soap to wash up
- Change the water frequently and rinse equipment under clean water to remove the soap bubbles
- Rubber gloves help you to wash in higher-temperature water, which is more hygienic

## Summary

Now that you have come to the end of this unit, you will have learnt that:
- a balanced diet is important for a person's health
- it is important for children that families have good eating habits
- some people have different food requirements and need special diets
- it is important to handle and store food safely to stop germs from causing illness.

# Chapter 17

# CFC 1 Confidence building for the young child through play

## What you will learn in this unit

You will gain an understanding of:

- activities that help a child to express their feelings
- activities that help to build a child's confidence
- the support a young child might need to gain confidence through play
- the encouragement a young child might need to express their feelings through play.

## Support a child to gain confidence through play 1.1

### Play activities to build a child's confidence

Activities for children can help to build their confidence. However, it is very important to make sure that the child has the right support from the adult, and that the activity is at the right level for the child's age and ability. A suitable activity is one that is neither too easy nor too difficult. For example, if the child is too young to hold a pencil and control the marks they make on the page, asking them to copy their name might damage their confidence and they may not want to try and use a pencil again. This activity may damage the child's confidence because they may feel that they are 'not

> ### Important words
>
> **Build confidence** – like a wall being built, confidence can be built up with the support of an adult.
>
> **Gain confidence** – when children develop more belief in themselves and what they are able to do.

**Figure 17.1** Children's confidence can be boosted by completing an activity successfully

good enough' or 'not clever', when actually they are just too young for this activity.

It is very important that when the adult plans the activity, they understand what each child enjoys doing. By including a child's interests in the planning, adults can give the child the chance to learn, at the same time as having fun doing something that they enjoy. Adults need to give the child the opportunity to learn new things and develop new skills, but they must make sure that the child can complete the activity successfully, as this will help to build the child's confidence.

## Supporting children to gain confidence in an activity 1.2

Supporting a child to gain confidence is a very important part of childcare. Adults can easily damage a child's confidence, and it is sometimes very difficult for a child to rebuild their confidence.

There are many ways that an adult can support children to gain confidence during play. It is very important that adults think about how to help children become confident. The following could be helpful:

**Figure 17.2** Adults can boost children's confidence by praising their efforts

- adults providing appropriate activities for the child

- adults providing suitable equipment for the child, such as suitable scissors

- giving the child praise and encouragement

- helping the child to do the activity if they are finding it difficult

- allowing the child to do it themselves if they can.

Children need to understand that it is all right to make mistakes, as this is part of how they learn. Their confidence can be easily damaged if they try something and are not good at it. They may feel embarrassed about trying again, so adults need to praise the child for trying and encourage them to have another go.

**Assessment task 1** ✓

Stevie is four and a half years old. List three activities that would be suitable to help build Stevie's confidence. Write down how the adult could support Stevie during the activity to help build her confidence.

## Encourage children to show their feelings through play

### Activities which support children to show their feelings

Some activities give adults the opportunity to support children's self-esteem. Examples are shown in Table 17.1.

**Important words**

**Express feelings** – show others how you are feeling.

**Self-esteem** – how you feel about yourself.

| Activity | The adult's role in supporting the child's self-esteem |
|---|---|
| Circle time | Adults should give every child the chance to talk about themselves and be listened to. This supports the child to feel valued and helps build their self-esteem. |
| Stories and books | Stories sometimes make children think about different feelings, so adults should take time to listen and comfort the child if they feel frightened, sad, or angry. Adults should also share in children's feelings of happiness and encourage this. This helps to build a child's self-esteem. |
| A trip to the shops | A trip like this can allow children to gain confidence in their ability to keep themselves safe; e.g. if children learn how to cross a road safely or walk sensibly along a path, they will be praised by the adults for learning about road safety. This will make them feel they are responsible and will build their self-esteem. |
| Giving children responsibilities | When children are given little tasks or responsibilities (such as pouring the juice or feeding the nursery rabbit), they feel proud of themselves, and this builds their self-esteem. |
| Painting and drawing | When children create pictures, they sometimes show their feelings. Children do not always think about what they are painting; they may just want to enjoy feeling the paint move on the paper or watch the colours mix. Adults should say 'Tell me about the picture' rather than ask 'What have you painted?'; this allows children to talk about feelings if they want to. The child will feel that the adult is interested, and this will support their self-esteem. |

**Table 17.1** Activities which can boost children's confidence

## Supporting a child's self-esteem ⓶⓵ ⓶⓶

Self-esteem is how you feel about yourself. Good self-esteem means that you have positive thoughts about yourself; for example, 'I will have a go, and if I make a mistake that's ok, I will try again.'

Our self-esteem suffers when we do not feel good about ourselves: for example, feeling 'I am not good at anything' or 'I always make mistakes so I am not going to have a go because I will get it wrong.'

### Task

In small groups, each think of something that you found difficult in school.

Think about how you felt: were you given good support and encouragement to try again, or were you criticised, and not confident to have another go?

Think about the support and encouragement you received from adults: did this affect how you felt about yourself?

Ways to help children build good self-esteem include:

- Learning the child's name and using it correctly, so that they feel you are interested in them.

**Figure 17.3** Children have a good chance to be listened to during circle time

- Adults always listening carefully when the child is talking. If a child tells you they feel sad, take the time to talk to them about these feelings, and try and comfort them.

- Showing the child that you are interested in what they are doing; for example, 'What do you most like playing with in the nursery?'

- Using supportive words and body language when talking and listening to the child; for example, smiling and saying 'What a lovely painting! Tell me about it.'

## Assessment task 2

Write down two activities for children aged three to four years, and say how the adult could support the child during the activity so that the child can develop good self-esteem.

## Summary

Now that you have come to the end of this unit, you will have learnt that:

- children's confidence and self-esteem can be developed by caring and supportive adults
- play activities are a very good way to build children's confidence
- some play activities give children the opportunity to talk about or act out their feelings
- children need to know that it is all right to make mistakes, as that is how they learn.

# Chapter 18

# CFC 2 Listening to and talking with a young child

## What you will learn in this unit

You will gain an understanding of:

- the skills that adults need to use when communicating with young children
- activities that will help to develop children's talking and listening skills
- the role of the adult in supporting talking and listening activities.

## Communicating with a young child 1.1

### How an adult can be responsive when listening to children

To listen to children properly, adults need to give them their full attention when they are speaking. Here are some tips for being a good active listener:

- Give your full attention to the child who is speaking. This will show them that you are listening and interested in what they have to say. This will encourage the child to talk.

- Do not look around the room when the child is talking to you. Make sure you look at them. Again, this will show them that you are interested and value them.

- Make sure your mind is focused on the child and what they are saying. It is easy to let your mind wander, and you may miss what the child is trying to say. This may result in the adult missing important information that the child is giving.

- Let the child finish speaking before you begin to talk. When you interrupt, the child may think that you are not listening, even if you are. The child may stop talking and move away.

- Use positive body language, such as nodding your head or looking concerned. This will let the child know that you are hearing what they are saying.

- Listen out for the main ideas and ask the child questions if you are not sure that you fully understand. For example, you might say 'How did you get to the seaside, on the coach?' or 'Tell me again about your sore leg.' This will help you to fully understand the information that is being given.

**Figure 18.1** It is important to listen to young children

## Assessment task 1

In pairs, with one person acting as the listener, the other as the talker:

- The talker can tell the listener about something important to them, such as what they did at the weekend, or their favourite television programme.

- The listener can use two ways to show the talker that they are interested and listening to what they are saying. An example is smiling or nodding the head.

- Write down the ways in which a person can actively listen to what somebody is saying to them.

### Active listening 1.2

Active listening is very important when caring for young children. When we are talking to people we often do not listen very well – we only think we do. Actually we may be only half listening!

Listening properly to children will help to make them important and well cared for; this helps them to develop good confidence and self-esteem.

If we do not listen carefully to children, they may feel unimportant, which could damage their self-esteem. They may be trying to tell you something that is very important to them. If this is ignored, the adult may be putting the child's life at risk; for example, the child may be trying to tell you that someone is hurting them and that they are worried.

### Important words

**Active listening** – when you listen carefully to a person who is talking, using body language to show them that you are interested.

**Body language** – how a person might stand, or the movements they make that show how they feel or what they may be thinking.

**Figure 18.2** Body language is important when working with children

As well as listening, good communication with children means that the adult needs to communicate well. Tips for communicating well with children:

- Speak clearly and try to pronounce words correctly. This will help children to speak correctly.

- Use simple sentences with young children so that they understand what you mean; for example 'Tidy up time.'

- Get down to the child's level and show positive body language; for example, stand slightly back to give the child space.

- Use appropriate facial expressions; for example, if the child is telling you that something is hurting, show concern through your facial expressions. You could damage a child's self-esteem if they feel that you do not care.

- Use open-ended questions. These are questions that do not encourage the child to give one-word answers such as 'yes' or 'no'.

- Use appropriate language. Always use words that support the child. NEVER swear or use bad language in front of the child.

- Never shout at a child. You should only shout if a child is in serious danger, such as walking too close to a moving swing.

## Important words

**Open-ended questions** – questions that are asked in a certain way so that the answer gives more information than just 'yes' or 'no'.

## Task

Read the following sentences: which ones are open-ended questions?

(Remember, these are questions that DO NOT require one-word answers.)

**1** Tell me about your new coat.
**2** Is your new coat warm?
**3** Did you do anything interesting at the weekend?
**4** What did you do at the weekend?

Write down two more open-ended questions that would be suitable to ask young children.

# Activities to support children's talking and listening skills ⟨2.1⟩ ⟨2.2⟩ ⟨2.3⟩

| Activity | The role of the adult | The child's role |
|---|---|---|
| **Books** (suitable for all ages) | • Choose a range of books for the age of the child. Picture books are suitable for young babies, and longer stories for older children.<br>• The role of the adult is to read the story well, using different voices for each character.<br>• Adults should always read the story first to make sure that it is suitable and that they can read all of the words.<br>• Listening to the children repeating words and encouraging them by saying 'well done.'<br>• Listening to children retell the story, and helping them if they forget what happens next. | • Allow the child to choose a book from the selection.<br>• Younger children could repeat sounds or words from the book.<br>• Older children can listen to the story, then act it out or tell it again in their own words. |
| **Circle time** (suitable for children aged four and five years) | • To organise a few children to sit in a small circle.<br>• Adults should explain the rules to the children; for example, 'We listen to each other and take turns to talk.'<br>• Give children the chance to talk; this could be about their favourite toy or what they did at the weekend.<br>• Listen to what the child is saying and remember the things they enjoy. | • Children to think about what they want to say and perhaps bring in a toy or object from home.<br>• Children need to listen to each other and follow the rules of circle time by taking turns to speak. |

**Table 18.1** Activities that will develop children's listening skills

| Activity | The role of the adult | The child's role |
|---|---|---|
| **Songs and rhymes**<br><br>(suitable for all children from birth) | • Learn suitable songs and nursery rhymes.<br>• Encourage the children to join in and learn the actions.<br>• Listen to the children when they suggest songs to sing. | • Children will listen to the song.<br>• Remember some of the words and repeat them.<br>• Try and learn some of the actions. |
| **A trip to the park**<br><br>(suitable for children aged three to five years) | • The adult's role is to plan a safe route to walk to the park and share this with other adults.<br>• Make sure there are enough adults for the number of children.<br>• Explain to the children where they are going.<br>• Tell the children about keeping safe.<br>• Listen to the child when they are telling you about what they enjoyed most. | • Listen carefully to instructions given by the adult.<br>• Talk about what they feel about the trip: happy, worried, etc.<br>• Ask questions so that they understand what they will be doing.<br>• Talk about the trip when they return. |

**Table 18.1** Continued

## Summary

In this unit you have learnt that:

- there are lots of skills that adults need to use when communicating with young children, including listening and taking an interest
- some activities are good for developing children's talking and listening skills
- adults can support children to be good talkers and to understand that it is important to listen to others.

# Index